Blessings
to Robbin ~
Angels
abide ~
Grace
Terry '10

PRAISE FOR *TEN SIMPLE STRATEGIES*

"This is a wise book. In every age, saints and sages speak to us in the language of their time. We benefit by letting their wisdom sink into our souls. Grace Terry has written this book in 21st Century language. Let it sink into your soul. You may benefit...tremendously."
-Bren Dubay, Executive Director and Covenanted Member of Koinonia Farm

"Ten Simple Strategies is a heart-touching and inspiring blend of insights, practices, and stories that reveal the beauty and grace that we all have within, so that we can contribute to a brighter future for all of us. We are each other's teachers, and Grace Terry shines her wisdom light on how we can live with more joy and sensitivity. Highly recommended."
-Will Tuttle, Ph.D., author of the best-selling book, *The World Peace Diet,* a recipient of the *Courage of Conscience Award*, the co-founder of Circle of Compassion, and an acclaimed pianist and composer. www.willtuttle.com

"Ms. Terry's warm and wise book makes profound spiritual and psychological concepts understandable and accessible. With humor, personal stories, and practical suggestions, she supports the reader through the process of personal transformation with gentle guidance and respectful, unconditional acceptance of each

individual's unique journey. Highly recommended — this book will be a faithful companion which will be referred to again and again."
-Anne C. Sulli, MA, Reiki Master, Interfaith Minister

"Grace speaks simple things in profound ways. Her wholehearted desire to make a difference through sharing experience, hope and wisdom shines throughout the book."
-Martha Creek, New Thought/Ancient Wisdom Teacher, www.marthacreek.com

"A lifetime of experience in a small book. Grace Terry provides you with stories, awareness exercises, and information to manifest a happier you. A must read for anyone wanting to change their life."
-James T McCallum Jr, Ed.D, University Dean (Retired), Transformational Coach and Motivational Speaker

"*Ten Simple Strategies* is a thoughtful guide containing simple, yet powerful steps that anyone can use to reclaim their happiness and lead a more fulfilling life. Readers will see glimpses of themselves in Grace's stories, and realize that they are not alone on their journey. Thank you, Grace for reminding us that peace begins when you forgive yourself and realize your inherent worth and value to the world."
-Laura J. Bauer, Executive Director, Mattie J.T. Stepanek Foundation

"Sister Grace., Thank you for sharing such a powerful and insightful piece of work. It is a mirror that enables one to seek inner peace before we can live with others peacefully. So grateful having the opportunity to have been part of this study."
-Rev. Jacqueline Johnson, Asst. Minister at Beulah Baptist Institutional Church, Tampa, Florida

Wow, what can I say? From the minute I started reading, I immediately started to feel better about myself and the world we live in. Grace has tapped into what we all need to read and hear for planetary healing. This brilliant and researched writer shares wonderful reminders, quotes, and insights that we can put into our daily practices to live the life we were born to live. Ms. Terry absolutely speaks of Great Things, Simply Told."
-Armand Della Volpe, published author, performer, inspirational speaker and award-winning singer/songwriter.

"Grace Terry's new book is a buffet of humor, deep empathy for human suffering, and simple-to-learn life skills to live a happier and more fulfilling life. I was charmed, warmed, and encouraged by this book. And her signature concept of the Rule of 51% has me looking at my behavior in a much more positive way!"
-Adele Michal, Abundance for All Coach, www.AdeleMichal.com

"Grace, thank you for sending me your manuscript. It is clear that you have shared a lifetime's worth of wisdom. Your book feels very empowering - you help folks believe that anyone can make a difference in themselves and thus all of us. Your focus on lifelong learning and re-learning of some lessons is a very important idea. And I really like the 51% rule - that if we just do something 51% of the time, we can have an impact. All the best,"
-Harriet R. Jardine, Ph. D. Psychology; retired faculty member from Middle Georgia State University

"This book rocks, as the children in my court would say! Ms. Terry identifies roadblocks which keep us from achieving happiness and tools to use in overcoming them. The book can be read and re-read, and new ideas can be gleaned with each reading. I intend to keep it close at hand. ... BTW, I really loved it!"

-Deborah Edwards, Juvenile Court Judge, Houston County, Georgia

"If you want to know what it's like to be a peacemaker, there no better way than to read Grace Terry's *Ten Simple Strategies*.... When journeying with Grace, you will enter a remarkably perceptive and prophetic introduction to become fully and wonderfully human in a world that desperately needs and welcomes the miracle you will have become."
-Dr. Andrew Harnack, author of *The Emptyful Chair: Journeying into God's Mystical Presence*

"...these *Ten Simple Strategies* are amazing, transformational, transcending and thought provoking and deserve great recognition and a place in libraries, schools, colleges, universities, mental health centers and home book shelves in this nation and around the world. ....The Minister/leader/servant has been still and has listened to a Higher Power and has spoken divine wisdom. *Ten Simple Strategies* is a tool kit for life's journey...."
-Rosa Mckinzy Cambridge, MMIN, RN, BSN, CM; President, National Black Nurses, Tampa FL; Past President, National Council of Negro Women Metropolitan Section, Tampa, FL; Board Member of Calvary Community Clinic; King Kids Consultant

TEN SIMPLE STRATEGIES FOR A HAPPIER YOU:

CHANGING THE WORLD FROM THE
INSIDE OUT

GRACE TERRY

CONTENTS

Ten Simple Strategies For a Happier You:
Changing the World From the Inside Out

By Grace Terry, MSW

Copyright 2020 by Grace Terry

DEDICATION

With great gratitude,

*I dedicate this book to all those
who have given me an opportunity
to practice transcending, overcoming,
and rising above adversity.*

*You have given me the opportunity to practice
being an overcomer instead of a victim.*

AND

*.... to all kindly and patient librarians everywhere,
especially the public and school librarians who helped me
as a child and adolescent to
become a lover of words and books.*

*As an adult you introduced me to women's music
that fed my soul during a particularly difficult time.
You helped me survive.*

*Did you even know that
you were doing suicide prevention?*

DISCLAIMER

This publication is designed to provide competent and reliable information regarding the subject matter covered. However, it is sold with the understanding that the author/publisher is not engaged in rendering financial, legal, psychotherapeutic, medical or other professional advice through this publication. If the reader requires expert assistance to address individual needs, the services of a competent professional should be sought.

The ideas/strategies/suggestions recorded here were gathered by the author over a lifetime of study, exploration, and seeking. Every word of this text is true in the author's personal experience. To emphasize: *not one thing* is included here except what the author has found to be true in personal experience. Your mileage may vary. Feel free to take what works for you and ignore the rest.

In compiling this content over forty-plus years of adulthood, your author regrettably did not always keep good notes of sources. Therefore, your author is not always able to cite a source for every statement. If the reader wishes to confirm or dispute anything included here, internet searches can be quite helpful.

Every effort has been made to make this volume as accurate

as possible. However, there could be mistakes or errors, both typographical and in content. Therefore, this text should be used only as a general guide and not as the ultimate source of information or direction. The ultimate Source of information and direction is found within each reader.

In the event you the reader use any of the information and/or suggestions in this book for yourself, which is your inalienable right, the author/publisher assumes no responsibility or liability for your actions.

ABOUT THE AUTHOR

Grace Terry (a.k.a., "Amazing Grace") received her Master of Social Work degree in 1980. She jokes, "Before I was a professional social worker, I was an amateur social worker. I was my family's first case manager by the time I was six years old....I've since resigned from that position."

Grace is a wise woman in the sacred tradition of the wounded healer. In transcending her own challenges with childhood abuse and neglect, multiple traumatic losses, clinical depression and anxiety, chronic pain and disordered eating/food addiction, she gained skills and knowledge she generously passes forward today.

In addition to having been a licensed mental health professional for over twenty years, she is now a mind/body/spirit wellness coach specializing in the management of chronic pain, whether the pain is physical, emotional, spiritual, or a combination of these. She is also a sacred storyteller, ordained interfaith minister, and an inspirational/motivational speaker.

Knowledgeable in many areas, her favorite role is that of grief educator/mentor/companion. With compassion, eloquence, humor and finely attuned intuition, she is a transformative channel for healing and peace in all of these roles.

Grace is the Founder of *Angels Abide Messenger Service*. By definition, angels are messengers. Grace is a messenger of messengers. While assisting clients, she is often used as a medium to receive and convey messages from heavenly angels (messengers from God) and spirit guides (the souls of deceased loved ones). She also brings divinely inspired messages through her writing, speaking, teaching, mentoring, and consulting.

Grace is available for individual, family, or small group coaching or consultation, for leading workshops and retreats, and for keynote speaking. Her fees are moderate and flexible. To schedule a personal consultation or discuss sponsoring an event with Grace, you can contact her through www.angelsabide.com.

FREE GIFT OFFER

Your author recommends journaling with specific assignments in order to receive the greatest benefit from these Ten Simple Strategies.

Some readers like to write. Others don't. If you are one who doesn't necessarily love to write, no worries! You get an A+ just for reading the book if you never put a single mark on paper.

However, if you are willing to put single words, phrases, doodles, sentences, and/or paragraphs on paper to get the most from this process, I want to make it easy for you. First, remember that no one will be grading your handwriting, grammar, your use of words, sentence or paragraph structure, *or anything else.*

Second, to receive a FREE download of convenient journal pages for all suggested journaling, contact Grace through www. angelsabide.com.

Having these suggested journaling assignments at the top of a fresh page will help you slide effortlessly into pouring your thoughts and your heart out in a transformative process that will astound you if you have not yet experienced the joyful power of journaling.

P.S. If you are not really very interested in becoming a happier person while making a real difference, don't do the journaling. (Tee hee.)

PREFACE

For as long as I can remember, I have had a passionate desire to make a positive difference with my life, to have my life *matter*, and to leave the world a better place because I lived. Perhaps many of you reading this book share this passion.

You may also share my very human struggles to be happy while making a difference. From adolescence through middle age, I struggled with clinical depression, severe anxiety, and a life-threatening eating disorder, all while becoming a successful mental health professional. My graduate education and professional licenses and certifications made me legally credentialed to provide mental health services, but what really made me a good therapist was the tenacious pursuit of my own personal peace through therapy, self-help groups, and spiritual practice.

Having transcended to a great extent my own challenges with the assistance of many wise teachers and helpers, I can now enjoy "passing forward" with great gratitude some of what has been most meaningful to me in my own journey. This book is a distillation of some of the most valuable lessons I have learned and relearned along the way. It grew from a talk I have given dozens of times over the years to many groups of both professionals and lay persons. Feedback has been universally positive.

By no means have I graduated from the lessons of Earth School. That won't happen until this life ends and I move on to whatever is next. I am still learning and re-learning these lessons. Each time I repeat a lesson, I integrate the wisdom at deeper and deeper levels of consciousness. Writing this book helps me to internalize the truths I share. It is all part of an on-going journey toward being the person I was born to be. One of my spiritual teachers said, *"We teach best what we most need to learn."*

For many years, my favorite quote has been this one from the great Irish playwright and Nobel Prize winner George Bernard Shaw:

> "This is the true joy of life – that being used for a purpose recognized by yourself as a mighty one. That being a force of nature, instead of a feverish, selfish little clod of ailments and grievances complaining that the world will not devote itself to making you happy. I am of the opinion that my life belongs to the whole community and as long as I live it is my privilege to do for it whatever I can. I want to be thoroughly used up when I die. For the harder I work the more I live. I rejoice in life for its own sake. Life is not brief candle to me. It's a sort of splendid torch which I've got to hold up for the moment and I want to make it burn as brightly as possible before handing it on to future generations."

Feel free to make this your favorite quote as well. Whether or not you make this your favorite quote, know that you matter, your life matters, and what you do with it is vitally important to the on-going evolution of humankind.

INTRODUCTION

THE POWER OF CHOICE

Life happens. Sometimes it hurts, but it doesn't have to hurt all the time.

Whatever happens, no matter how painful or difficult, we humans all have choices as to how we respond. As conscious beings, we can choose thoughts and behaviors that build resilience and make it possible for us to bounce back from life's painful challenges and be happy.

DEFINITION OF HAPPINESS

For our purposes here, let's agree that happiness is an overall peace and satisfaction with one's self and one's life. Being happy overall doesn't mean we never feel sad, frustrated, fearful, or ashamed. Being happy means we safely and thoughtfully express and release those painful feelings within a relatively short time then focus on more positive aspects of life in order to be at peace again.

Simple, right? Yes, simple, but not necessarily easy, especially if our training in the earth school up to now has *not* included the idea that we *always* have choices about how we think and choices about how we act and react. These choices largely determine our feelings, which to a great extent determine our quality of life.

Some readers may resist the idea that we have the power to *choose* thoughts, feelings, and expressions (that is to say, our state of consciousness) at any moment. Please don't let this be a stumbling block if, at this time, you aren't completely convinced this is true. Put the issue of choice aside for now to be revisited later at your convenience. There's much of value for you in this volume, whether or not you completely agree with this concept. Please just continue to read with an open heart and mind and remember throughout the book to take what works for you from this book and overlook the rest.

Choosing happiness can also be hindered if we've never learned that *all our feelings are acceptable and honorable.* We can "process" them, which means we feel them, express them safely, learn their lessons, and then release any pain while retaining the lessons.

Unfortunately, most of us learned early in life the erroneous idea that some of our feelings are bad or unacceptable and shouldn't be felt, much less expressed. As a result of this erroneous training, we deny, ignore, or otherwise repress normal, appropriate feelings. The result is emotional constipation.

Instead of feeling and releasing emotional energy, we travel through life carrying a heavy toxic load of unprocessed emotions that no longer serves us. This backlog of emotional sludge can prevent us from enjoying happiness in the here and now, just like unprocessed or undigested food stuck in the colon can poison the whole body and wreak havoc on our physical, emotional, and spiritual health. (Have you ever tried to be pleasant, happy, and spiritually focused while constipated?)

The good news is that all of us humans were born with an innate ability to feel our emotions, express and release them safely, receive comfort as needed, and return to a state of peaceful joy. We *all* need comforting sometimes and there's plenty of comfort available to us. We each have the ability, with practice, to create nurturing, mutually supportive connections to others who can and will give and receive comfort as needed. We can also learn to nurture and comfort ourselves in appropriate, powerful, life-enhancing ways.

If you haven't yet learned to consciously make choices about thoughts, actions, and reactions OR if you haven't yet learned to honor and process your emotions OR if you haven't yet learned to create a loving comfort network of companions, know this: If you're willing to learn these things, this book can help you.

This book is NOT a substitute for therapy or spiritual practice. If you have struggled for any significant period of time with feelings of sadness, unworthiness, anxiety, guilt, or resentments or have unsuccessfully attempted to cease self-defeating behaviors, consider seeing a professional therapist and/or consider participation in a self-help or support group. There needn't be any shame in seeking help. Typically, our deepest wounding involves other people. Also typically, our deepest healing involves other people, often a combination of mental health professionals, enlightened clergy, and peer companions on the pathway. Neither wounding nor healing happens in isolation.

Whatever you have learned or believed in the past can be updated, adjusted, or modified to fit and work better for you now and in the future. In the meantime, congratulate yourself for surviving and for doing as well as you've done so far. Forgive yourself for any mistakes you have made in the learning process up until now (more on forgiving self and others in Chapter 6). Congratulate yourself for reading this book. Know that your best days are still ahead!

MIND/BODY/SPIRIT

As you use this book, remember there's no separation in health of body, mind, and spirit. Any factor that affects *any* of these dimensions of the Self will simultaneously affect *all* of these dimensions for better or for worse. Making choices that affect the Self negatively in any way affects the body, the mind, *and* the spirit negatively. Correspondingly, making choices that affect the Self positively in any way will affect the body, the mind, and the spirit positively.

I like to think of the word *robust*, which means strong and effective in all or most situations and conditions, in relation to happiness and health. People living in robust good health and happiness acknowledge and develop their strengths and find positive ways to compensate for their limitations and vulnerabilities, often by including in their personal network selected companions who have strengths that complement their challenges.

It's important to remember than even the strongest, happiest people sometimes *feel* weak or sad. All humans have limitations and vulnerabilities and all of us have times when we're acutely aware of our limitations and vulnerabilities. Feeling weak or sad or afraid doesn't make us weaklings or failures or cowards. Feeling worthless does NOT make us, in fact, worthless. It's just a feeling and if we let it, the feeling will pass. Feeling weak or sad or afraid or worthless at times only means we are human.

....AND WHAT'S THIS ABOUT CHANGING THE WORLD?

At the time of this writing, we live in a complex, gorgeous, glorious, fast-paced, challenging world that seems to get smaller and smaller. The twenty-four-hour news cycle and mass media advertising and entertainment constantly bombard us with stimuli that are often distressing and, in fact, are dangerously toxic if not filtered. How can one individual make a positive difference? The answer lies in the concepts of *individual consciousness* and the *collective consciousness*.

INDIVIDUAL CONSCIOUSNESS

Each individual, at any moment, can be said to be vibrating energetically at a particular level of consciousness. Synonyms for the term *level of consciousness* include:

- a mental attitude
- a state of mind
- a mind set
- a worldview
- a perspective
- a frame of mind

Various states of consciousness can be imagined along a vertical continuum. At *higher or lighter* levels of consciousness or vibrations, the individual

- chooses,
- experiences, and
- expresses

thoughts and feelings that reflect, for example,

- unconditional love (for self and others),
- joy,
- optimism/hope,
- clarity,
- compassion/kindness,
- acceptance of self/others/situations (an attitude of "it is what it is " without resentment, worry, regret, or criticism)

- empathy,
- serenity,
- transcendence (rising above anything that might disturb one's serenity)
- a sense of harmony and oneness with all that is, and
- similar positives.

At lower, darker, slower vibrations or levels of consciousness, the individual

- chooses,
- experiences, and
- expresses

...thoughts and feelings that reflect, for example,

- negative judgment (criticism), of self and/or others
- blame,
- neurotic guilt (guilt which no longer serves a useful purpose),
- anxiety/fear,
- pessimism/fatalism,
- confusion
- hatred of self and/or others,
- depression,
- hopelessness/despair,
- frustration,
- outrage, and
- similar negatives.

NO VALUE JUDGMENT ON CONSCIOUSNESS

It's important to remember that states of consciousness aren't morally good or bad. Rather, states of consciousness are simply an attitude or frame of mind that the individual chooses (consciously or unconsciously), experiences, and expresses at any particular moment. Expressing a "bad attitude" (lower, darker/slower energy) doesn't make one a bad person and vibrating with a "good attitude" (higher level of consciousness) doesn't, in and of itself, make one a good person.

All of us are spiritual beings on a human journey and all are innately lovable, valuable, and worthy whatever attitude or state of mind we might be experiencing and expressing at any particular moment. Humans are *born* essentially lovable, valuable, and precious and we never outgrow that, no matter what we do.

However, higher levels of consciousness typically *feel better* and increase our subjective enjoyment of life. Also, vibrating at higher levels of consciousness improves measurable indicators of mind/body/spirit health, such as blood pressure, organ functioning, blood sugar levels, and so forth. An individual's chosen mindset or perspective (that is to say, state of consciousness) can fluctuate subtly or radically from minute to minute, hour to hour, day to day, year to year.

We may make a moral judgment or a value judgment when lower, darker energy is expressed in *behavior* that's destructive of one's self and/or others. However, we remember that the person acting destructively is a *spiritual being on a human journey and is, therefore, good,* albeit confused, misguided, wounded, or otherwise challenged.

We may judge *destructive behavior* to be inappropriate rather than negatively judging the inherent worth of the one behaving destructively. We can hold people accountable for their inappropriate destructive behavior without labeling the person as "bad." (Again, if this is an idea with which you cannot completely agree at this time, set it aside for now to be revisited at your convenience.)

COLLECTIVE CONSCIOUSNESS

Each *individual's* state of consciousness contributes to the *collective state of consciousness* at any moment. If the individual is vibrating at a lower, darker, slower level of energy, that individual is contributing to a collective consciousness of darkness. Manifestations of collective lower energies include what may be called social or societal problems (for example, crime, poverty, discrimination, mental illness, alienation, xenophobia, and others), which are all rooted in fear, anger, shame, and/or sadness.

If an individual is vibrating at a relatively high level of consciousness, that individual's energy is helping to neutralize and transform lower, darker energies and, thereby, is contributing to the salvation/healing/ongoing positive evolution of humankind. They're part of the solution to what are known as social problems.

HIGHER CONSCIOUSNESS MORE POWERFUL THAN LOWER

Up to this point in the history and evolution of humanity, higher levels of consciousness have been more powerful in transforming and neutralizing lower, darker energies than the reverse. Otherwise, the human race would have completely self-destructed by now. At times, we came perilously close to total obliteration of life as we know it, but higher energies prevailed.

It's easy to be overwhelmed by negative stimuli and sink into hopeless, helpless despair over the state of the world in which we live. *Always remember this:* anything (no matter how seemingly small or slight) that an individual does to become happier and healthier raises that *individual's* vibration or state of consciousness and, thereby, helps to neutralize and transform lower, darker energies and raise the *collective* consciousness.

So there's no reason to feel that you're being selfish when you pursue your own mind/body/spirit wellness. In so doing, you're simultaneously improving the well-being of all humankind. *We are all connected.*

Fred Rogers, the immortal creator, composer, writer, puppeteer, and host of *Mr. Rogers' Neighborhood,* alluded to this idea when he said, "Imagine what our real neighborhoods would be like if each of us offered, as a matter of course, just one kind word to another person. There have been so many stories about the lack of courtesy, the impatience of today's world, road rage and even restaurant rage. Sometimes, all it takes is one kind word to nourish another person. Think of the ripple effect that can be created when we nourish someone. One kind empathetic word has a wonderful way of turning into many."

BE A SUPERHERO!

Mr. Rogers definitely vibrated at a high frequency and was a "Superhero" in raising the collective consciousness. *The message of this book is that anyone can be a Superhero in raising the collective consciousness by doing some relatively simple things to become happier as individuals.*

FILTER THE NEWS

To be a Superhero requires an awareness of the effect of the twenty-four-hour commercial news cycle and its influence on the individual and the collective consciousness. To be considered "newsworthy," an incident typically must be unusual and out-of-the-ordinary. For example, a recent daily national news broadcast reported that 73,000 consumers in Manhattan were suddenly without electric power in a blackout that lasted for several hours. This resulted in widespread panic and fear of a terrorist conspiracy.

The news report on the day *before or after* the blackout did *not* say, "Electric power is working well with normal efficiency today in Manhattan and all is well..." If listeners had heard something so mundane on a national news broadcast, we would have next heard about the firing and replacement of the News Director. Understandably, normal efficiency in Manhattan or anywhere else was not considered newsworthy the day before or after the blackout and wouldn't be considered newsworthy on any day.

Keep in mind when you are exposed to commercial news media that you're always hearing what's *unusual.* Unless we put the reported news in this context in our state of consciousness, the commercial news media can, on its own, drag us down into lower, darker, slower vibrations of chronic hopelessness and despair.

I came to the awareness that "news" is by definition "the unusual" several years ago and have spoken about this many times to people who seemed to be negatively impacted by what they were hearing on news broadcasts. I offered this perspective as a way to instill hope and mitigate the sense of helplessness and hopelessness I sometimes observed.

THE DALAI LAMA SAYS...

Then I discovered the following quote by no less a luminary than His Holiness the Dalai Lama, who said:

"We humans have existed in our present form for about a hundred thousand years. I believe that if during this time the human mind had been primarily controlled by anger and hatred, our overall population would have decreased. But today, despite all our wars, we find that the human population is greater than ever. This clearly indicates to me that love and compassion predominate in the world. And this is why unpleasant events are "news"; compassionate activities are so much a part of daily life that they are taken for granted and, therefore, largely ignored."

So, with all humility, I believe that His Holiness would concur when I recommend you limit your exposure to news reports funded by commercial interests as well as to mass media advertising and mass media entertainment, which are always aimed at the lowest common denominator of the target group of consumers. Rigorous scientific research has documented that both news reporting and advertising have lasting significant impacts on the states of consciousness of both individuals and the collective. Certain entertainment programs can be as detrimental to the psyche as news reporting and advertising.

ACTION STEPS

As a healthier alternative to commercially sponsored news reports, do a search of organizations that are making a positive difference and, therefore, are raising the collective vibration. (One excellent well-known example is Habitat for Humanity, which has made huge progress in eradicating homelessness, but there are countless others.) Follow them on social media and/or subscribe to their newsletters. You'll hear good news that you would most likely never hear otherwise. Make at least a small monetary donation to those organizations to support their work and to express appreciation for the fact that they're inspiring all of us to a higher level of consciousness and are, thereby, helping all of us. By making a financial donation no matter what size, you will be personally invested in the work of the organization and that will help to raise YOUR level of consciousness as well as that of the organization's! I promise you will feel great about it!

CHOOSING OUR FOCUS

Whatever we focus on expands. If we focus on a problem, then the problem expands. If we focus on being part of the solution, the solution expands.

The kind of actions/reactions that are saving humankind typically aren't reported on the news and aren't illustrated in advertising. They're so common as to be considered ordinary. However, if we, as individuals, notice and acknowledge the redemptive behaviors of others and set our intentions to generate positive influences ourselves, this planet and its inhabitants will be evolving for future generations.

Again, to quote the beloved Fred Rogers of *Mr. Rogers Neighborhood* as he reminisced,

"When I was a boy and I would see scary things in the news, my mother would say to me, 'Look for the helpers. You will always find people who are helping.' To this day, especially in times of 'disaster,' I remember my mother's words, and I am always comforted by realizing that there are still so many helpers – so many caring people in the world."

Notice how Mr. Rogers focused his awareness on the positive, even in the midst of situations that can be called disasters.

THE BOTTOM LINE

Anyone can make a positive difference in themselves and, thereby, in the ongoing evolution of humankind. Anyone reading this book has set an intention (consciously or unconsciously) to be part of the solution, contributing meaningfully to raising the collective consciousness. The ten chapters of this book give specific, simple yet powerful strategies that have been life-changing for me. I believe with all my heart that the suggested strategies can be life-changing as well for you the reader if you truly wish to be happier and healthier in mind, body, and spirit and therefore part of the evolution of humankind.

Jane Addams, the first American woman to win the Nobel Peace Prize (1931) and the mother of my profession (social work), writing about her *Twenty Years at Hull House,* said, "People did not want to hear about simple things. They wanted to hear about great things – simply told." My humble intention in sharing these strategies is to speak simply about great things.

A MENU, NOT A LIST OF THINGS TO DO...

Beloved reader, as you scan through these chapters suggesting ten simple strategies to be happy while making a real difference, please do not assume that this is intended as a list of tasks for you to complete perfectly in a limited period of time. Rather this is a list of gentle suggestions intended to spark your imagination.

Scan through the chapters lightly. Then choose one or (if you must) two strategies from the ten chapters to *play with* rather than *work on*. Play with this first one or two chosen strategies for at least a week or two, a month, or several months before choosing another suggestion or two with which to play.

By all means, make it fun! *Don't* make it a compulsive pursuit of perfection. That totally defeats the purpose. Perfectionism is NOT happiness. In fact, it is self-sabotage of the highest order and be sure that I know this first-hand!

RULE OF 51%

You don't have to use any of these ten strategies perfectly in order to increase your happiness and raise the collective consciousness. In fact, I have a principle I call the "Rule of 51%," which simply means there's a tipping point in consciousness. It's the point where you are following positive happiness-enhancing practices an *average* of 51% of the time on a day-to-day basis. One day you may do 40% and the very next day could be a 65% day. The average of the two days would be 52.5%.

When your *average* consistency rate is 51% or higher over time, you'll find a noticeable difference in your subjective experience of life. You'll be noticeably happier and healthier in mind, body, and spirit. This subjective more positive experience of life can often be measured and documented with common testing procedures, such as blood pressure readings or simple standardized questions measuring overall happiness.

FIND YOUR PEEPS!

To have the most fun and get the most benefit from this book, invite several people to secure their own copies of the book and play along with you. Meet regularly and make the meeting a time that group members anticipate with joy. Talk about your experience with the strategies. It's okay if different people are playing with different strategies at the same time.

The point of getting together is to have fun, to give and receive support, and for each person in the group to hold him/herself accountable to the group. Notice that I say each group member can hold themselves accountable to the group. This is completely different from the group attempting to hold the members accountable.

Spiritual beings on a human journey will absolutely do things with accountability and support that they will never do alone. However, as self-responsible adults we voluntarily *choose* (there's that word again) *to hold ourselves accountable* rather than relegate ourselves to the infantile position of having others hold us accountable. Expecting others to hold us accountable is a set-up for frustration, resentments, and power struggles that will only drain the energy of the individuals in the group and the energy of the group as a whole.

Each person can give a personal status report at each meeting and ask for any particular type of support needed. Leadership or facilitation of the group can rotate so that no one is identified as "The Expert" or "The Boss." That's not fun for anyone. Encourage everyone in the group to share the blessings and lessons of servant leadership. (If you are not familiar with the principles of servant leadership, do a brief internet search on this term. It's not rocket science.)

JOURNALING AS A TOOL

Another way to get the most benefit from this "Ten Simple Ways" adventure is to keep a journal of your experiences with the strategies Start with a clean, fresh notebook, date it, and jot down your thoughts, feelings, and "ah-ha" realizations as you play with one or more strategies. Then enjoy looking back through these notes from time to time.

Handwriting, grammar, spelling, and sentence/paragraph construction *do not matter* in your personal journal. What matters is your honesty and authenticity, which can be achieved by writing from the heart. The best way to do this is by writing for a predetermined period of time (could be five, ten, twenty minutes...) faster than your mind can edit and don't stop writing until your time is up. Consistency is valuable, but an average of one note every week or so is better than none. *You cannot do this wrong.*

With some of the ten strategies, a journal is more important than with others, but with any of them a journal can be a simple yet powerful tool. Make notes in your journal about day-to-day successes, learning and relearning opportunities, and challenges you encounter as you make a sincere effort to follow each suggestion.

THE POWER OF COMPANIONSHIP

If the idea of gathering a group of people together to explore the ten strategies with you seems daunting, I highly recommend recruiting at least one partner who will acquire their own copy of the book and read it along with you, sharing their experiences along the pathway. I repeat for emphasis: *for most (and perhaps all) spiritual beings on a human journey, when we hold ourselves accountable to at least one other person and give and receive unconditional support from at least one other, we'll do things that we'd never do alone. We are not wounded in isolation and we do not heal in isolation.*

You and your accountability partner(s) can hold yourselves accountable to one another in the following fashion (or in any fashion that works for you):

Agree that you will have regular contact and specify how often, allowing for some flexibility in unusual circumstances. Make contact with one another a high priority in your life.

Agree on your usual medium of communication, whether face-to-face, on-line meetings, phone, skype, email, social media messaging, or whatever works best.

Your partnership can begin with a time-limited agreement (for example, "We will communicate weekly for eight weeks") OR can be open-ended. Often, an initial commitment of six to eight weeks works best. At the end of the first committed time, a new commitment can be negotiated or the same one renewed. Initial agreements can be renegotiated at any time as needed.

When you communicate with your accountability partner(s), give a self-report of instances since your last communication in which you've had a learning experience with your chosen suggestion. Report lessons you learned or relearned in the process. Let the lessons learned or re-learned be the focus of your communications. *Lessons learned or relearned are always a success.* Reporting on challenges is optional.

Give one another *unconditional* affirmation, applause, congratulations, kudos, empathy, and support for even setting the intention of becoming happier and healthier in body, mind, and spirit and, thereby, making a difference and raising the collective consciousness.

Don't give advice to one another. Advice is generally unnecessary and ineffective. If one or the other partner asks for advice, perhaps the most helpful response could be to *wait, breathe*, and *then* and *only then* say something like, "Tell me what you have already tried or thought of trying.... What do you think is the best thing for you to do? ... I hear that this is tough for you. ... I believe in your ability to work this out."

THE POWER OF LISTENING

If a partner is struggling with challenges and shares those challenges, sometimes the most helpful response is to say, "I hear you... How can I help?" Don't be surprised if they answer, "You're already helping just by listening." Believe that you are really are helping simply by listening. You are giving a priceless gift.

Many times, the person who is struggling needs only to be heard. When someone listens, the speaker can verbalize their way into finding their own solution to the dilemma. Don't be too quick to offer answers or remedies. When serving as an accountability partner (and in other situations as well), *often the best and only necessary response is, "I hear you," assuming that these words are spoken sincerely along with nonverbal cues that express genuine caring.*

HIGHER AND HIGHER

Happy, healthy people enjoy the upwardly spiraling pathway day by day, rather than being fixated humorlessly on the destination. So, take a deep breath and let it out, smile, and buckle up!

Chapter 1

CELEBRATE YOUR TALENTS, GIFTS, AND STRENGTHS

EVERYONE HAS TALENTS, GIFTS, AND STRENGTHS. SOME PEOPLE are better at owning them, developing them, and showcasing them, but that doesn't mean that some people have them and others don't.

THE TRAP OF PERFECTIONISM

Unfortunately, in the culture of the Western industrialized world, most people learn to be perfectionists and believe "until I'm perfect, I'm worthless..." Too often, we learn to be self-effacing and hypercritical of ourselves. We tend to focus only on mistakes, flaws, faults, and difficulties and never learn to enjoy or take any credit for our positive qualities. This is a set-up for defeat and misery in life and, taken to extremes, can lead to life-threatening, self-destructive practices.

Many extremely successful people have little to no self-worth because they obsess only about their perceived faults or imperfections. No amount of "success" (as measured by fame, wealth, achievement, or recognition and/or affection from others) can compensate for this self-defeating, often preconscious mindset.

Depending on your generation, readers will recognize the names of Sylvia Plath, Billie Holiday, Marilyn Monroe, James Dean, Elvis Presley, Hank Williams, Sr., Jimi Hendrix, Janis Joplin, Whitney Houston, John Belushi, Michael Jackson, Kurt Cobain, Karen Carpenter, River Phoenix, Robin Williams, Anthony Bourdain, and others. We have no way to know for sure, but could it be that these are examples of extremely talented people who drove themselves unmercifully into early deaths because they wouldn't acknowledge to their deepest Selves their own worth?

Also consider such gifted people as Lindsey Lohan, Tiger Woods, Robert Downey, Jr., and Charlie Sheen, who, thankfully, are still students in the "earth school," but whose painful struggles are well known. I mention all these names with absolutely no negative judgment or criticism, but with sadness at the loss to the entire human family when souls as brilliant as any of these act self-destructively. I repeat for emphasis: *We are all connected.*

To be happy and healthy in mind/body/spirit, we can learn to acknowledge and appreciate inherent talents and strengths and capitalize on those, while making efforts to improve in other areas of our lives where improvement is needed. In order to celebrate and enjoy our innate strengths and talents, we first clearly identify them.

TIME FOR JOURNALING

In your journal, first make a list of what you think may be your greatest attributes or talents. Don't sell yourself short. Write down what you do well. You don't have to be the best ever at something to put it on this list of things you do well. Just write down the things that perhaps come easier to you than to some others and/or things that at least one person has noticed and complimented you on.

It might be relatively simple things, like being punctual most of the time, being patient, being good with animals, or ... *anything at all!*

Also, write down the positive qualities that you express on your best days. You don't have to exhibit a positive quality 100% of the time in order for you to include it on your list. For example, if it's true that most of the time you're friendly, write "friendly" on your list.

Again, don't sell yourself short. If you question whether or not to include a particular quality on your list, give yourself the benefit of the doubt and write it down.

If you struggle with negative ideas about your physical appearance or your body image, the following is absolutely mandatory. This may be way outside of your comfort zone, but do it anyway. Write down things about your body or your appearance that you appreciate. It can be something as simple as "my heart beats automatically without me thinking about it" or "my lungs, kidneys, liver, stomach, eyes, ears, nose, and brain function and serve me well."

Find things about your appearance you can put on the list of things you appreciate about yourself. This may require that you look in the mirror with new eyes.

For example, as a child and adolescent, people often told me I had beautiful blue eyes. It was true. I had inherited them from my handsome, blue-eyed father. However, when I looked in the mirror, all I could see was that my eyelashes were pale, short, and sparse. I agonized daily over my lack of long, thick, naturally curled eyelashes. I spent excessive time, money, and effort on eye makeup in an effort to create the illusion that my eyelashes were fashionably long, dark, thick, and curled.

At some point in my adulthood, as I was learning new things, I realized that, in fact, I *did* have beautiful blue eyes! I had never seen them before!

So, look in the mirror (with new eyes if necessary) and list at least one or two things about your physical being (sometimes called the body temple) that are positive. (More about this in Chapter 3.)

Then find several people who know you well and who have demonstrated a capacity to be kind and helpful. Tell them you're making a good faith effort to follow the suggestions of this book and you need their help. Ask them to tell you what they think are your best personal qualities and what they think you do well. Put all of those things on your list.

Don't reject anything that someone else gives you. If you feel doubtful about some of the positive feedback you receive, ask the person giving it to tell you a specific example of a time you did that thing well or demonstrated that quality. Then write it on the list.

CELEBRATE!

After compiling this list, begin to brainstorm ways that you can celebrate these talents, gifts, and strengths. Make this into a list of possible ways to celebrate your positive qualities. Add to the list as you create additional possibilities. HINT: In my experience, the greatest way to celebrate gifts, talents, and strengths is to find fun ways to share them with others.

Choose one or two "celebration ideas" from the list - the ones that you think would be the most fun and positive for you, even if they draw you outside your comfort zone. Then play with these ideas. Don't work on them. Play with them!

Practice giving as much mental and emotional energy to positive ideas about your gifts, strengths, and talents as you give to your perceived weaknesses or imperfections. Play with finding fun ways to celebrate and/or share these good qualities.

THE RULE OF 51% APPLIED HERE

When you receive positive feedback about your celebrations (which you will), just pause, breathe, breathe, breathe, and let the good energy soak into your skin, your brain, your heart, your midsection. You will become a happier, healthier person. When your positive thoughts about these attributes reach an average of 51% as compared to negative ideas, your world will change. Try it and see for yourself.

Don't worry if this all feels awkward or silly, especially at first. What's the worst thing that could happen? Just do it anyway, if not for yourself, then do it for the entire human family. It will get easier with practice.

In completing these action steps, you will inspire others to celebrate their own talents, gifts and strengths. Doing this will give others the motivation and the permission to do the same. The positive ripple effect will help to raise the collective vibration of the entire planet. We are all connected!

Chapter 2

CHOOSE THOUGHTS THAT ATTRACT HAPPINESS AND HEALTH

THIS SUGGESTION IS SIMPLY A BROADER APPLICATION OF THE principles in Chapter 1. In addition to adjusting our ideas and beliefs about our strengths, gifts, and talents, we can become happier and healthier when we consciously practice choosing thoughts that are life, health, and happiness enhancing.

A BELIEF IS A THOUGHT WE KEEP ON THINKING.

Our brains are so efficient that, often, our thought patterns happen outside of our conscious awareness and are called "subconscious" by many. I prefer the term *pre-conscious* because these thoughts, ideas, and beliefs can be brought into our conscious awareness just by slowing down and paying attention.

When a thought becomes internalized as a belief in our conscious or pre-conscious mind, changing it can take time and practice. For some, changing negative beliefs may require participation in a self-help peer-support group or help from a professional coach or therapist or enlightened clergyperson. Again, spiritual beings on a human journey can achieve goals with support and accountability that they'll never achieve alone.

We don't form life-limiting beliefs in isolation and, typically, we don't change them in isolation. That's no reason to be embarrassed or ashamed. That's simply how humans are "hard-wired," to use a technical term. To use less technical terms, we humans are created to thrive in mutually beneficial relationships with other humans and, in fact, with all sentient beings and (some say) with the whole Universe. None of us can expect to thrive in isolation.

THINK ABOUT WHAT YOU'RE THINKING ABOUT

We can start the process of changing thought patterns by becoming ever alert to what we're thinking not only about ourselves but also about other people, life, and how the world is working. For example, some of us constantly think/believe things like "Everyone is out to get me," "It's a dog-eat-dog world," "Nothing ever works out for me," or "I've been cursed from the beginning." Rigorous scientific research has shown that thinking and believing these things can negatively impact not only a person's mental/spiritual health but also their physical health.

Take all the time you need to play with this one suggestion before moving on to others. There is no need to rush through this. Changing our thought patterns can take significant time, energy, and consistent effort. Do not expect yourself or anyone else to make radical changes in thought patterns overnight. Making radical changes too quickly could be totally disorienting. *Easy does it – but do it!*

In order to change our mental activity to more life-enhancing patterns, we start by simply noticing our thought patterns. Then as we are ready, we begin to substitute alternative thoughts that are more likely to build us up rather than tear us down.

A PERSONAL EXAMPLE

Here's an example from my personal life. In 1984, I was thirty years old and immature emotionally and spiritually. My beautiful, vibrant, fifty-six-year-old mother was killed suddenly in an automobile accident. For many years afterward, I told myself, "No one will ever love me the way my mother loved me...." Every time I had that thought I would feel newly bereft, hopeless, and completely alone.

Finally, one day I thought the negative thought, felt horrible, and *noticed* what I had done. On the spot, I decided to change the thought to something like, *My mother still loves me, and other people also love me without condition.... I am lovable and I feel my mother's love and support right now.... Even though she has physically left the earth plane, the very best of my mother is still with me. Her love and support are eternal and are as close to me as my very heartbeat... Thanks, Mom, for your love and support while you were here on this earth and up to this very moment.... I love you back!*

As the reader might imagine, these thoughts created a very different outcome for me in measurable happiness and mind/body/spirit health. I eventually reached a point in my journey where I came to think and believe (with humility, gratitude and absolutely no arrogance or vanity or feeling of superiority) that *"the whole Universe loves me without condition."* I am saved from arrogance and superiority because I also believe that the Universe loves *everyone* without condition - and that idea deserves another book all to itself!

THE RULE OF 51% APPLIES HERE

When 51% of your thoughts are life-affirming and life-enhancing, your world will change and you'll become noticeably happier and healthier. As you continue to notice and adjust your thinking about everything, you'll experience a better and better quality of life.

Some may say, "But it's not that simple...." How do you know how powerful this one suggestion can be unless you try? What do you have to lose, except being unhappy and unhealthy?

When your new positive self-talk occupies your mental space

an average of 51% of the time, you will have advanced lightyears into a new dimension that will continue to get more and more joyful and fascinating. At the same time, your higher, lighter consciousness will be helping to raise the collective consciousness and making the world a safer home for all.

JOURNALING

Jot notes in your journal as you discover self-sabotaging ideas and beliefs and be sure to write down the more life-affirming ideas and beliefs that you want to gradually internalize. Share these jottings with your accountability partner(s). You can get affirmation and support as you courageously play with this suggestion. That will make it more fun and easier and will accelerate your progress toward a happier, healthier you.

Chapter 3

LOVE YOUR BODY WITHOUT CONDITION

OPT OUT OF BODY LOATHING

A VARIETY OF FACTORS HAVE CREATED A CULTURE OF BODY loathing in the Western industrialized world. Body loathing feeds the industrial machine, which produces products called health and beauty aids to make the human body "acceptable," and drives the mass market advertising industry, which helps to create insecurities so that more money is spent on the products. However, body loathing has significant damaging effects on the individual and, by extension, on families, communities, and the entire ecosystem of the planet. Needless to say, body loathing lowers the collective consciousness.

A BIT OF MY STORY

I reached adulthood with a deeply ingrained sense of disgust and revulsion about my physical being, fueled by the shame, guilt, and fear-based patriarchal religion of my childhood. I purchased enormous quantities of "beauty aids" and personal hygiene products as well as clothing and accessories in order to *look good on the outside*, be acceptable, and gain approval from others.

Somehow, it never worked. I never looked good enough. That is to say, I never looked like the women on the covers of the fashion magazines and in the advertisements or the women starring on television or in the movies.

All the while I was desperately trying to perfect my outward appearance, I was abusing and neglecting my precious body temple. I started dieting at an early age and, by adolescence, had a full-blown eating disorder. I knew little or nothing about appropriate self-care.

Eventually, some very wise people helped me realize, first of all, that neither the "cover girls" nor the "flavor of the week" media starlets looked like the images that were force fed into my consciousness. It was all an optical illusion!

Every image on the cover of a magazine or in the ads was created by a small army of professional illusionists (makeup artists, hairstylists, wardrobe coordinators, lighting experts, photographers, graphic artists, and others). The stars of the small and large screens all had their own entourage to help them achieve the desired illusion on screen and on the red carpet - at least temporarily. It was a world of make believe and total superficiality. I realized that unless I chose to devote my entire life to the pursuit of the perfect visual image, I would never achieve the look created by the professional illusionists.

Wise people also helped me to understand that beauty, health, self-esteem, and sex appeal come in all shapes, sizes, colors, ages, and textures, regardless of what images make it onto the cover of this month's *Seventeen, Cosmopolitan,* or *Woman's Day* magazine (or into the centerfold of Playboy). I learned to see true beauty, both inner and outer beauty, in myself and in other real people. It was there all the time, just waiting for me to open my eyes, my mind, and my heart to discover it.

I also learned to treat my body temple lovingly in terms of the nutrition I ingest and the movement I enjoy. All of this has been a lifelong learning and relearning process for me and continues to this very day. I have been blessed to receive *lots* of help in this process. I didn't get shamed and deluded in isolation, so I didn't try to get better in isolation.

LOVING MY BODY TEMPLE

I can now honestly say that I love every single cell of my body, even the fat cells! My body has served me faithfully in spite of all the years of neglect and abuse. My body keeps my soul and spirit grounded on the earth plane. Since I'm here, I assume that this is exactly where I most need to be right now!

As a conscious adult, I now acknowledge and appreciate the infinite miracles of my physical body. My senses, my organ systems, my organs individually, and even the individual cells of my body function incredibly well all the time without me even giving much thought to it! I don't have to remind my heart to beat, my kidneys and other organs to work, my ears to pick up sounds, or my balancing mechanisms to hold me upright.... All of this and so much more happens smoothly with little or no planning or effort.

I wholeheartedly reject the notion that there's a very narrow ideal of beauty and health and that anyone (including me) who doesn't meet that ideal is a failure or somehow less valuable than those who do somehow meet today's standard. I also reject the idea that young is beautiful and age is not. I also reject the runaway consumerism necessary in order to pursue ideal (that is to say, youthful, trendy) beauty. This insanity is literally destroying the planet and many individual lives in the process.

WHO SAYS....???

If enjoying any level of self-appreciation and self-acceptance regarding your physical being seems like an impossible dream to you, start by questioning everything you've ever been told about your body - what it should look like and how it should work for you. Then begin to notice all the things that your body temple does to serve you.

My beloved uncle lived into his nineties in relatively good health - physically, emotionally, and spiritually. As he aged, he developed some chronic health concerns. Around age ninety, his personality completely changed. He became grumpy, harsh, and even rude at times. His whole demeanor was downcast. When I gently questioned him, he blurted out, "*I have four things wrong with me...*" and then he named them. Yes, they were all matters of concern and every one of them was a challenge to manage. Fortunately, he had excellent insurance coverage, excellent health care providers, and a devoted family to assist him.

Rather than being grateful for the life force still within, he was spending most of his waking hours ruminating morosely on those *four things* that troubled him. He refused to acknowledge that anything was working well! He became very depressed (though he refused to admit that) and spent the last several years of his life thoroughly miserable himself and making others uncomfortable as well.

YOUR LIFE FORCE IS GREATER

Whatever physical challenges you may have, if you're reading this book, your internal, inherent life force is greater than any lower, darker energy (ailment, injury, pain, or dis-ease). Otherwise, you wouldn't be alive. Start doing things that will nurture, nourish, and strengthen the life force flowing throughout your physical being.

BREATHE, BREATHE, BREATHE.

A simple beginning is to get still, get quiet, close your eyes, and just notice your breathing. There's no need to change it, but it may change without effort as you pay attention. Just *notice* the air coming into your nose and down the back of your throat and down into your lungs. Relax and exhale through your mouth. Do this several times and appreciate this simple miraculous rhythm of life. Let your mind be still for a moment or two as you breathe and just appreciate your body temple and all its wondrous glory. If you do nothing else but repeat this one-minute practice regularly, it will make a difference in the subjective experience of your mind/body/spirit health and happiness.

JOURNALING

Start a list in your journal of things you love and appreciate about your body temple. Focus on what is working well for you. Be constantly aware of any little or big thing about your physical being that is positive in your experience. Keep adding to the list as you become more and more adept at noticing and appreciating the miracle of your body.

Be creative in discovering new ways to nourish and pamper your physicality. Find healthy ways to enjoy your sense of smell, taste, touch, hearing, and sight. You deserve it!

MAKING A DIFFERENCE

If you will gradually add to the conscious time you spend appreciating your body temple, your world will change significantly. You will become happier and physically, emotionally, mentally, and spiritually healthier. At the same time, you'll be elevating the collective consciousness and benefitting all of creation.

Chapter 4

PRACTICE GRATITUDE

EVERY ONE OF US HAS ANY NUMBER OF MANIFESTATIONS OF good fortune in our lives. Consciously cultivating an attitude of gratitude will increase the flow of good into our lives. Also, gratitude saves us from toxic self-pity, which is the very antithesis of happiness and health. Some wise person observed, "Gratitude is a natural anti-depressant."

I'll never forget a young woman who shared her gratitude at a support group meeting I attended many years ago. She said, "I am so grateful that I've had a shower today. Not long ago, I was living on the street and had no way to take a shower. Now, I usually take two showers a day, and I'm so grateful for my warm showers." I often think of this young woman when I take my warm shower, and I'm very grateful.

MY MOM'S RADICAL GRATITUDE

My mother was a great teacher of gratitude. No matter what difficulty she might be facing (and she faced many), she always looked for blessings and she always found them! This practice helped my mother through many hard times, and she was happier and healthier for it.

Mother had a small decorative plate hanging on the wall in her kitchen which read:

"Thank God for dirty dishes,
They have a tale to tell.
While other folks go hungry
We're eating very well.
With home, health, and happiness
We shouldn't want to fuss.
For by this stack of evidence,
God's very good to us."

Can you look at a stack of dirty dishes and give thanks? Are you willing to learn?

AS SIMPLISTIC AS THIS MAY SEEM...

Start by being grateful for being alive. Your life force is greater than your death instinct, or you wouldn't be alive. Be grateful for your body, all of its intricate miraculous systems, and all of your senses. Pause for a moment before each meal and be grateful for your food and for all that nourishes and sustains you.

Be grateful for every teacher (even your ex-spouse if you have one...) and for every learning experience you've ever attracted and co-created. Be grateful for the beauty of nature, for art, for music, for books and the ability to read. Be grateful that you live in the most prosperous, most enlightened age ever known to humankind.

Unless you're dying of starvation and exposure, drawing your last breath (in which case you would not be reading), you have some means of support and sustenance. If you have any income or source of support, no matter how limited it may seem, be grateful! Being grateful for what you're now receiving will open the channels for you to receive more.

If you have debts and bills to pay, be grateful to every one of your creditors! The Universe has trusted you and has loaned you goods and services for your convenience. Be grateful for every check you write and every bill you pay.

APPRECIATE YOURSELF!

Appreciate your strength; it's there or you would never have survived to this point! Appreciate your own beauty. (*Everyone* is uniquely beautiful. The more you acknowledge and appreciate your own beauty, the more you'll also appreciate the beauty of others.) Appreciate your creativity. Appreciate your generosity and your ability to love.

Appreciate your perseverance. You've never completely given up, even though you may have been tempted many times. (If you had given up completely, you wouldn't be alive and reading this book.)

Appreciate your sense of humor. It's there or you would never have survived to this point! (More about this in a later chapter.)

Appreciate your divinity. *You are a spiritual being on a human journey.* (More about this in the chapter on celebrating your spirituality.)

APPRECIATE OTHERS

Lavishly express your appreciation verbally to those who contribute in any meaningful way to your life. For example, from time to time I attend banquet-style gatherings of various groups. I try to always express my appreciation to the wait staff. (I was one of them when I was working my way through graduate school.) I make eye contact and say to them, "Thank you for coming to work today...." It seems to make a difference to them, and it definitely makes a difference *to me!*

Openly acknowledge your gratitude to the people who have

made a positive difference in your life. Let them know you appreciate them. Make a habit of writing thank you notes.

JOURNALING

Begin making a list of the people who have had a positive impact in your life. Write down as many as you can remember, and continue to add to the list as you remember others. Write at least one thank you note or gratitude letter to one living person who has made a significant positive difference for you. Mail or deliver the letter to them. If the person who has made the most impact on your life is deceased, write the letter anyway. Read it to someone you trust who can appreciate and support your efforts.

For thirty days, write down in your journal at least five things a day for which you can honestly say, "I am grateful." Be very specific. It doesn't have to be anything huge. It can be the simplest, smallest thing. What matters is that you consciously acknowledge to yourself that you're grateful for these things.

Once you've written one thing down on your gratitude list, don't write it down again. Find five new things each day. As you go through your day, be consciously aware of new things you can add to your gratitude list.

Again, this doesn't have to be done perfectly to be very powerful. If you skip a day or more, just start again as soon as possible. If it takes you three months or more to write down five gratitudes for thirty days, so be it. Just do the best you can to be consistent for thirty days. Give regular progress reports to your accountability partner(s) as you complete your thirty days.

MAKING A DIFFERENCE

When you've done this for thirty days, you will have developed a habit of looking for examples of good fortune in your life and finding them. This habit alone can make you measurably happier and healthier and can elevate your individual consciousness enough to make a difference in the collective consciousness. You're evolving and you're making a difference for the entire human family!

If you have any doubt as to how powerful your gratitude can be for the entire human family, I have one story from my personal experience to share.

A PERSONAL STORY

Many years ago I was working as a social worker for a community agency. My duties took me on occasion to a community health clinic which served low income families.

One morning, I walked up the sidewalk toward the front door of the clinic. Just as I opened the door from the outside, a short, round, middle-aged, black lady arrived at the door from inside the clinic. I automatically stepped aside, held the door open for her to exit the building, and said, "Good morning, how are you?" She smiled and in a sweet voice exuding gratitude and good cheer, she replied, "I'm BLESSED, Baaaaybeee!" as she stepped out the door and floated by.

Operating on autopilot, I stepped inside the clinic and let the door close behind me. I stood still just inside that door for several moments. I was absolutely stunned by the positive energy radiating from that woman's being. I could feel the energy of her genuine gratitude vibrating in every cell of my body! I have not been the same person since. In a moment, I was changed forever.

It took several years for me to begin to integrate the impact of that brief encounter into my heart and mind and spirit. I'm still in the process of integrating it.

I have told the story on many occasions in many different settings. Judging from the non-verbal responses, many listeners don't really get the message, but a few in each audience do understand and resonate. I'm okay with that. If even one person in an audience gets it, then it is worth telling. Every time I tell the story, I get the lesson again, at deeper and higher levels.

...and now when someone asks me how I am doing, more often than not, I smile and say enthusiastically "I'm BLESSED, Baaaaaybee!" (I'm now at a wonderful age when I can call just about anyone "baby" without offense.) My prayer is that at least once in my lifetime, I might have the impact on someone else that the beautiful short, round, middle-aged, African-American angel had on mine.

Are you willing to have a life-changing impact on another individual life and a redemptive influence on the collective consciousness? If so, just pick your method. Gratitude is only one pathway. This humble volume gives you ten.

Chapter 5

CELEBRATE YOUR SPIRITUALITY

"We are not human beings having a spiritual experience,
we are spiritual beings having a human experience."

THIS QUOTE HAS BEEN ATTRIBUTED TO THE FRENCH philosopher Pierre Teilhard de Chardin, but its authorship has never been confirmed. Well known authors and teachers like Wayne Dyer and Steven Covey have popularized the quote and the attribution. Whatever wise person first said this was onto something.

CULTURAL CONTEXT

My formal education and training are in the field of social work, which teaches that the individual can only be fully understood in the context of their culture, including cultural institutions such as family, government, education, and religion. In this manuscript, I've mentioned more than once the negative influence of Western industrialized culture on individual and collective measures of happiness and health.

I can also say that there are many positive ideas/thoughts/practices embedded in our culture. The positive aspects don't need to be examined, challenged, overcome, or transcended in order to be happy and healthy. Consequently, they don't get much attention in this manuscript.

It's enough for the reader to know that I'm not "anti-everything" related to Western industrialized culture. While appreciating and enjoying the positive benefits of our culture, I hope to be a positive catalyst for ongoing cultural evolution toward greater individual and collective happiness and health.

I say all of this at the beginning of this chapter because in the realm of spirituality, Western industrialized culture overall is sadly immature and decidedly confused. Certainly, there are in the Western world countless spiritually mature, enlightened people helping to raise the collective consciousness of the entire human family. However, the historical legacy of shame/fear/guilt-based patriarchal religion and our blind avaricious pursuit of material gain still seem to me to dominate the culture of the so-called developed Western world.

ANOTHER BIT OF MY STORY

I grew up in a very religious environment that was extremely sexist, racist, and generally tainted by toxic shame (the internalized idea that "I'm not good enough. ... I am hopelessly/horribly defective, flawed, inadequate, sinful, damaged, broken, cursed, too much this and not enough that...").
I tried desperately to make that religion work for me and to be "good enough" (meaning perfect), all while trying to be "pretty enough," according to impossible standards (remember from an earlier chapter?) No matter how hard I tried, I failed miserably to reach that impossible dream of pure perfection.

By adolescence, I was an honor student, active in extra-curricular activities and looking for all the world like a well-adjusted young lady. However, I was slipping further and further into clinical depression, anxiety, and a full-blown eating disorder.

In order to survive, I walked away from organized religion as a young adult. I no longer believed nor wanted to believe the religious dogma I had been taught all my life. Not until years later would I become willing to do the inner work to clarify for myself what I *did* believe.

At age thirty, I experienced three traumatic losses, including sudden unemployment, a totally unexpected divorce, and the sudden death of my vibrant, beautiful fifty-six-year-old mother in an auto accident. Just a few years later, my fifty-eight-year-old father dropped dead of a heart attack, I went through a second divorce, and I was diagnosed with a life-threatening illness. It became a high priority for me to find answers to questions like,

- Is there a difference between spirituality and religion?
- Is there a Higher Power in the Universe?
- If there's a Higher Power, who or what is that Power and what are the qualities and characteristics of that energy?
- What does that Higher Power have to do with me and with my life?
- Is there a meaning and purpose to life in general and my life in particular?
- Why am I here?
- Who are all these other people and what do they have to do with me?
- What happens when this life is over?
- Are there universal spiritual principles that I can practice so that I can have a healthy, happy life?

I SEARCHED INTENSELY and am grateful to say that I was led to answers to my questions that worked at the time and continue to work for me now. The remainder of this chapter is devoted to my best attempt to articulate the ideas and beliefs that literally saved my life. I share these for whatever they may be worth, *and*

I encourage each reader to search for answers that work for you. Your answers might be very different from mine and I'm quite comfortable with that. I could be wrong or misguided. If so, I am seeking further enlightenment and always teachable. It could also be true that our answers are very different yet we might both be right!

THE DIFFERENCE BETWEEN SPIRITUALITY AND RELIGION

First, there's a definite difference between spirituality and religion. Let's review the quote at the beginning of this chapter. Every person is a spiritual being on a human journey. Within each person is a divine spark, an essence that is eternal, infinite, and divine. The Quakers call it "The Light" and say that it's the Light of God within every soul. Throughout recorded history, renowned and revered teachers of various faith traditions have taught this idea.

I choose to believe that every human being (and possibly every other sentient being as well) is spiritual, whether or not that being is involved in the active conscious practice of religion. Spirituality is inherent or inborn within all people and within all of creation. The difference between people is *not* whether they're spiritual but whether they're *consciously aware* of a reality that's metaphysical (that is to say, literally, beyond the visible physical reality).

Some people are more consciously aware of spiritual realities and/or may be operating more consciously with intention according to universal spiritual principles, such as

- love,
- acceptance,
- honesty,
- faith,
- surrendering to win,

- willingness,
- restitution,
- perseverance,
- humility (that is to say, being teachable),
- sanctification, and
- service.

THESE PEOPLE MAY or may not be affiliated with organized religion. If they aren't affiliated with any organized religious body, we could say that they're spiritually conscious but not religious.

Every religious tradition has people who may or may not be consciously aware of spiritual/metaphysical reality and who may or may not be operating according to higher spiritual principles. People within religious groups who aren't consciously aware and *not* operating according to universal spiritual principles are religious but not particularly spiritually aware.

I speak from experience when I say that religious practices, at best, enhance one's conscious contact with spiritual reality and, therefore, are life-enhancing, empowering, and healing. I also speak from experience when I say that, at worst, religious practices can be horribly damaging to individuals, families, communities, and societies to the point of being life-threatening and life-limiting.

Spirituality without organized religion is still spirituality. Religion (whether organized or not) without spirituality is empty at best and toxic at worst. These two complementary ideas are true whatever the particular religious faith or practice.

Respectfully, I submit that, in my mind and in my experience, there's a *huge* difference between spirituality and religion. In order to be healthy and happy, it may be important to the individual to consider this distinction. Again, I encourage each reader to decide whether or not this is an important issue for him/her and if so, whether now is a good time to devote personal time, energy, and effort to exploring this issue.

SEEK YOUR OWN ANSWERS

If you decide this is important for your health and happiness, I encourage you to actively seek answers and trust your Inner Wisdom to lead you to the truth that works for you. *Always trust the process! Actively explore and trust.*

In Asia, ancient wisdom teaches, "When the student is ready, the teacher appears." In my own journey, teachers have appeared to me as books, movies, television and other mass media, workshops, humans, animals, nature, angels, art, and in many other forms. Pay attention and remain teachable and you'll find the answers you seek.

HIGHER POWER?

I find validity in the idea that there's a Higher Power (a.k.a., God, the Force, Spirit, Creator, Allah, Father/Mother/Divine Child, Original Source...) in this Universe that's continuously and infinitely creative, positive, evolving, loving, and respectful. My concept of Higher Power includes both Father AND Mother AND Divine Child. Metaphorically, if Higher Power is Father, then Higher Power is also Mother and Divine Child. This idea is embedded in ancient sacred scriptures from many faiths (including Christian scriptures), often hidden in plain sight.

I was a devoted lifelong student of ancient scripture and never heard of or noticed the Divine Feminine/Great Mother until well into adulthood when I was led into reading feminist theology. The patriarchal teachers and texts I had known until then worshiped a false idol that was exclusively male and masculine and taught me to do the same. This was one of the many tenets of my early religious training that didn't work for me.

As I studied feminist theology, my concept of the Divine morphed into a very different image than the one to which I had previously been exposed. The more inclusive image of the Holy Family worked much better for me.

The existence of a Higher Power is certainly debatable, and I could make the case for atheism probably as convincingly as I can make the case for believing. I just know it works better for me to believe. Your mileage may vary.

A MODERN PARABLE

If you are debating internally as to whether or not anything in the Universe could rightfully be called God, consider the following story (adapted from a pamphlet that I highly recommend titled *Keys to the Kingdom: Five Fundamentals of Truth,* published by Unity Books).

As two soldiers prepared for battle, they discussed their deepest personal beliefs. One was a man of faith and the other was an avowed atheist who said, "One thing this war has taught me is that there is no God!" The believer said quietly, "This war has taught me that my only hope in this life or the next is the mercy and grace of God...."

Later, after the battle, the same two soldiers looked out over the human carnage left by hand-to-hand combat. The atheist challenged pointedly, *"Where is your God now?"* At that exact moment, a stretcher-bearer ran out to rescue a wounded comrade. The believer pointed to the stretcher-bearer and said, *"There goes God now...."*

Personally, I believe that I live, move, and have my being all within the Energy called "God" (by some). Every cell of my body vibrates with Divine Energy. I also believe that every cell of *every*body vibrates with Divine Energy. Every atom of everything in the Universe vibrates with Divine Energy. *Everything is connected*, and everything is divine in its origin and evolution.

THE PURPOSE OF LIFE?

Each person has not only the opportunity but the responsibility to decide for him/herself the purpose and meaning of life. There's nothing "out there" or "up there" or "over there" that decides the purpose for the individual spiritual being on a human journey. Each person can ask, explore, and answer the question for him/herself with absolute confidence that those who sincerely seek meaning and purpose find it.

The purpose of my life, I've decided, is joy, and part of my joy is helping others to experience joy. Writing this book is a chosen part of fulfilling my life purpose. Other ways include coaching/teaching/speaking, particularly in the areas of spirituality, grief education, and grief mentoring (watch for my next book!).

A major lesson that I selected for this lifetime is the lesson of spiritual partnership. I am supremely grateful that my current husband and I have recently celebrated our Silver Wedding Anniversary and have co-created a functional, joyful partnership. It's an ongoing curriculum with its own joys and challenges.

Aside from my marriage, I strive to co-create other mutually beneficial partnerships that serve The Highest Good of All. Again, this is an ongoing adventure with its share of challenges and seemingly an important part of the curriculum for me in this lifetime in the earth school.

WHAT'S NEXT AFTER THIS LIFETIME?

I personally believe that a conscious reality exists beyond this lifetime. Again, I could probably just as convincingly argue that what we call death of the body is the absolute end of the individual, period. My decision is to believe that within every person is a core essence that transcends the death of the body. In my worldview, the Spirit within every individual is eternal, infinite, and divine. That idea works for me.

The poet Wordsworth wrote:

> *Our birth is but a sleep and a forgetting:*
> *The Soul that rises with us, our life's Star,*
> *Hath had elsewhere its setting,*
> *And cometh from afar:*
> *...But trailing clouds of glory do we come*
> *From God, who is our home...*

While this idea stated so gorgeously by the poet works for me, you're free to decide what works for you. If you do decide to celebrate your spirituality, your options for doing so are infinite, and you get to decide which options to pursue!

JOURNALING

Here's one way to begin. Start two new pages in your journal and write the following questions at the top of a page (one question per page):

> "What can I do that will make me more consciously aware of and strengthen my connection to the Highest and Best *within me, within nature, within other humans, and/or within all of creation?*"

AND/OR ask yourself,

> "How can I practice spiritual principles today, *such as love, acceptance, honesty, faith, surrender, willingness, restitution, perseverance, humility (being teachable), sanctification, and service* in a way that serves the Highest Good of All?"

After having written these questions, take a deep breath, let it out, and start writing. Don't edit, censor, or criticize what flows from your heart through your writing instrument. Just write until your Inner Wisdom signals that your writing is complete for now. You can repeat this awareness/discovery opportunity as often as you wish.

Your journaling may stimulate a list of options or possibilities for celebrating your spirituality. Choose one or two and create an action plan with a target date. *Go for it.*

If you sincerely ask these questions and follow the guidance of your Inner Wisdom, you cannot possibly do it wrong. I would only encourage you to make it fun. Fun, for you, may turn out to be exploring various spiritual pathways or groups (either face-to-face in real time or online), taking classes (for credit or not, on-line or in an actual classroom), reading spiritual literature, organizing or choosing and advocating for a noble cause, spending time in nature, rescuing animals, volunteering for community service work, creating art and/or being inspired by other artists' works (including visual arts, language arts, performance art...), becoming a stand-up comedian....

WHAAAAAATT? Becoming a stand-up comedian?

Sure! Why not? Comedians make people laugh and that's holy work in my opinion. (We'll soon come to the chapter on keeping and cultivating a sense of humor). If comedy is created with the intention of serving the Highest Good of All, then it would certainly qualify, in my mind, for a celebration of spirituality.

INTENT AND CONTENT

Certainly, some comedy is nasty, vicious, and degrading to all who participate.... The difference is in the *intent* and the *content*.

Almost anything can be a celebration of spirituality, depending on the *intent* and the *content*. A student asked the master, "What is life before enlightenment?" The Master replied, "Chop wood. Carry water."

"So, then," asked the student, "what is life after enlightenment?" The master said again, "Chop wood. Carry water."

One can carry water and chop wood with gratitude and loving purpose or with grumbling, resentment, and self-pity. Same task, different intent, different consciousness or state of awareness.

Whatever one does can be an expression of spiritual intention and/or spiritual principles to serve the Highest Good of All – or not. The following is an example of this principle.

A medieval pilgrim trudged through the forests of Europe for days without seeing another human soul. By nature friendly and gregarious, he became very lonely. By and by, he neared a village and was thrilled to see a workman ahead. The traveler excitedly approached the workman, hoping for nothing more than a few minutes of pleasant conversation. He greeted the workman, "Hello there! What are you doing?"

The workman barely looked up before snarling back, "What does it look like I'm doing, you fool? I'm cutting stone."

Taken aback, the pilgrim responded, "Well, you certainly don't seem very happy about that...."

"What's to be happy about?" the worker snapped. "This is hard, hot, dirty work and everything I earn goes to feed a harpy wife and a house full of brats. I'll be working until the day I die and then it will all be over. What's it to you, anyway? Be gone before a rock falls on your head!"

The pilgrim hurried away disappointed but soon brightened as he approached another worker. More slowly and carefully this time, he approached and spoke to the second worker, "Hello there, what are you doing?"

The second worker looked up, smiled, put out his hand, and replied, "Hello there, pilgrim. I'm cutting stone, making a living for my family."

The pilgrim shook the second worker's hand and observed,

"That looks like hard, hot dirty work...You must get very tired doing it."

"Oh, sure, I get tired," said the stonecutter. "But at the end of the day, I go home to a wonderful wife and children... I'm just so happy and grateful to have a way to earn a decent wage so that my family can have a roof over their heads, clothes on their backs, and food in the supper pot. My family never goes to bed hungry. I'm a very lucky man."

"Well, good day, then, kind sir. I'll let you get back to your task. Give my best to your missus," said the pilgrim as he waved and moved along the village pathway.

Soon, he spied one more stonecutter along the way. Hoping to have at least one more human contact before the pathway led him back into the forest, he approached cautiously. "Hello there," he called to the third worker, "I see you're cutting stone."

"Well, yes and no," said the worker with obvious joy and excitement. "I'm cutting stone, but more important, I'm building a cathedral! People will come from all around to worship together here. They'll get strength and comfort and inspiration from being here in this magnificent structure. It will be most wonderful, and I get to help build it! I may not live long enough to see it finished, but just having a small part in building it is a great honor."

"Well, very good, then" said the pilgrim. "And how about your family? Are they proud of your work?"

"Oh, sure, I guess so," said the worker, smiling. "And I'm certainly glad that my building this cathedral is helping to feed and house and clothe my family. But long after I'm gone and my children's children are gone, this cathedral I am building will be here giving shelter and comfort and strength to families all around. I am most greatly blessed to be a part of this holy mission...."

YOUR SPIRITUAL LEGACY

In whatever you're doing with your life, are you cutting stone, making a living, or "building a cathedral?" Are you building something with your life that has a higher purpose, something of lasting value? What legacy will you leave behind when this life is over? You'll definitely leave something behind. The question is, *"Will you leave something behind that makes a positive difference?"*

You could be happier and healthier if you ask yourself the "Big Questions" (like those listed earlier in this Chapter), then create a plan that's enjoyable for you and makes a positive difference for others. You can be actively involved in the ongoing evolution of humankind and immediately help to raise the collective consciousness. Start exploring, knowing that one person with positive intentions and the courage to explore can make a *big* difference for themselves and for others. Be assured that *you cannot do this wrong*.

Chapter 6

PRACTICE FORGIVING
YOURSELF AND OTHERS

PROBABLY EVERYONE WHO USES THIS BOOK HAS BEEN TOLD AT one or more times that they *should* forgive. Unfortunately, very few have ever been taught or shown how to do forgiveness work. I'm about to tell you *how* in simple terms that anyone can use and understand. The only requirements are willingness and a conscious decision to release and clear out old, negative energy so that something new and fresh and life-enhancing can flow into that psychic space. This process is sometimes called forgiveness.

This suggestion alone can completely transform your life if you're willing to do the work. Admittedly, this is deep, intense inner work. At times, it can be painful, almost like undergoing surgery for a malignancy. Those who are willing to do forgiveness work find it to be worth the effort.

Refusing to forgive ourselves means we're holding onto toxic guilt and shame. Refusing to forgive others means we're holding onto resentments. Some anonymous wise person said, "Holding onto resentments is like drinking poison and expecting someone else to die." Resentment and guilt can literally poison a person's body/soul/spirit, shorten a life, and diminish a person's quality of life significantly. The saddest part of this truth is that these dire consequences are totally unnecessary.

The purpose of forgiveness is to take back your personal power. As long as your energy is being drained by guilt and resentments, your power to create happiness and health is significantly limited.

FORGIVING SELF

In consideration of forgiving yourself, first let's clarify the difference between guilt and shame. Guilt is feeling bad about *something I did*. Shame is feeling bad about *who I am*. Guilt says, "*I made a mistake.*" Shame says, "*I AM a mistake.*"

Guilt can serve a useful, short-term purpose. When I violate my own sense of integrity or violate my own moral code, healthy guilt tells me immediately that I've wandered off the true pathway. It's like a warning light that tells me to make a mid-course correction immediately. Healthy guilt is an indicator of a healthy functioning conscience, which is necessary for living productively among other humans.

If I listen to this healthy guilt, I can make my correction, get back on course, and make amends or restitution for any harm I've done. At this point, the healthy guilt has served its purpose and can then be released. Neurotic guilt hangs on long after it has served any good purpose, punishing and poisoning indefinitely.

Every human being has done things they later regret. It's part of the human experience. The healthy healing process when we make a mistake is to:

1. Admit our mistakes,
2. Make corrections,
3. Make amends or restitution when possible,
4. Learn or relearn the lesson(s) available,
5. Let go of the guilt, and

6. Move forward with new learning or re-learning.

Remember that when forgiving, you *aren't* condoning the mistake(s) you or others made. You *aren't* saying, "It's okay that I (or others) did this hurtful wrong thing." Instead, if you're the one who made the mistake, you're saying, "I'm willing to admit my mistake, make amends/restitution as best I can, learn from my mistakes, then (and only then) release the guilt so that I can be free today. I'll remember the lesson of this mistake as I move forward and do my best not to repeat it."

If another person made a mistake that was hurtful or costly for you, by forgiving them, you *aren't* saying, "It's okay that this other person made this mistake." Instead, by forgiving, you're saying something like, "I'm willing to release any negative energy I'm carrying that is associated with this mistake... Since I sometimes make mistakes and wish to be forgiven, I'm willing to forgive... I refuse to carry toxic resentment with me any longer... I'm not a victim. I'm an overcomer... What is the lesson to be learned or relearned in this situation? I'll remember the lesson, release the negative energy around this, and move forward in peace."

It sounds simple, does it not? It *is* simple. It's not necessarily easy. Many simple things aren't easy. *It's as difficult as we make it.*

This process may be difficult for some of us because we've never seen it modeled. Unfortunately, this simple process isn't widely understood or practiced in our culture. What's more commonly practiced is a defensive refusal to admit (and therefore learn from) mistakes and/or the neurotic, clinging self-flagellating guilt that serves only to keep a person stuck in spiritual poverty, pain and self-imposed victimhood.

The good news is that *anyone* can learn to *use* healthy guilt in a constructive, life-enhancing way and then *let go of it*! Like everything else, it gets easier with practice.

TOXIC SHAME

Unlike guilt, shame serves no useful purpose. Shame is a lie. It says to us, "You're worthless... You're not good enough... You're inadequate... You're stupid... You're ugly ... You didn't just make a mistake, you *are* a mistake... You're bad... You're broken... You're flawed... You're defective... You're evil... You don't deserve anything good... You deserve to suffer and to be miserable," and on and on and on.

We in the industrialized Western world live in a shame-based culture, a legacy of our historically shame-based interpretation of religion. All of our societal institutions (schools, churches, workplaces, government, and families) reinforce shaming ideas and perfectionistic standards that no human can attain.

Additionally, when children or immature adolescents and adults are traumatized and don't receive appropriate emotional care, the trauma can be internalized as shame. The person who has experienced trauma often responds with thoughts such as, *I must be an awful person for something this awful to happen to me....* Some even think, *God is punishing me for being such a sinful person....*

A third basis for shame is that anyone who doesn't reach the top 1% of the citizenry based on their net worth is considered not rich enough and therefore is a failure in a materialistic, consumption-driven world. The rule is that one can never be too rich or too thin....

Which brings us to another basis for shaming – virtually anyone who does not attain *this year's* "look" is considered inferior and for decades this year's look for women is extremely thin to the point of emaciation. However, no matter how thin or fashionably beautiful a woman may look, she's still a woman and, therefore, subjected to a certain amount of shame simply for having been born female.

People of color are shamed because they're not Caucasian. Differently abled people (sometimes called disabled) are shamed because of their abilities challenges. People of diverse sexual orientations are shamed because they're not heterosexual.

The sad news is that virtually every person alive today who grew to adulthood in Western industrialized culture has some degree of internalized shame, even if they are male, heterosexual, in the top 1% according to net worth, and this year's *People Magazine*'s Sexiest Man Alive. (NOTE: This may also be true of those who reached adulthood in other cultures, but I cannot speak to that with any degree of self-confidence.) The good news is that shame can be released and healed. As conscious adults, we can learn to live in the truth.

THE TRUTH AS I UNDERSTAND IT

The truth about us is that we are *all* spiritual beings on a human journey. *We are good enough*, in all our imperfect glory! We were born precious, lovable, and valuable *without condition*. We deserve every good thing the Universe has provided for us, which is infinite.

Again, you might say, "But it's not that simple!" I say, "It *is* that simple!" ...and releasing internalized shame is absolutely necessary if we are ever to enjoy robust happiness and mind/body/spirit health.

I also would say that releasing shame is typically a process, not an event. It can take time. If so, that's not a problem. We have plenty of time to do the personal evolution work we're willing to do. Often, people doing shame-release work need lots of loving support. If so, that's fine, too. There's plenty of loving support available to those willing to ask for support and accept it.

SPECIAL POPULATIONS

Survivors of child abuse and/or neglect, people recovering from addictions, women (also known as "the marginalized majority"), people of color, differently abled people, people of size, and LGBTQI people often need an extra measure of support. That's only because typically they have been given an extra measure of shaming! Needing an extra measure of support isn't a problem. There's *extra* support available to anyone who's willing to receive it.

The temptation with forgiveness work is to avoid it, skip it, or make cursory, superficial efforts that have no real results. Of course, these are options for anyone. If the reader truly wants to increase happiness and health, take your forgiveness work seriously and make a sincere effort to be completely honest and thorough. The results will be well worth the effort.

THE RULE OF 51%

You may be wondering, "Do I have to be 100% free from all of my old guilt and shame before I can enjoy greater happiness and health?" The answer is no. Again, the 51% rule applies. When 51% of your guilt and shame is released, you'll notice a significant increase in the quality of your life. You'll want to continue that healing process, but be assured that your forgiveness process doesn't have to be perfectly complete to enjoy abundant good health and happiness.

INVENTORY WORK

Next, I describe a powerful method for forgiveness that has worked exceedingly well for me. I'm about to describe a process called inventory work that you may or may not be willing to experience. Be assured, there's more than one right way to do forgiveness work.

If, after reading the remainder of this chapter, you aren't willing to give inventory work a fair trial and if you truly want to be free of guilt and resentments, take a few minutes to become still and quiet. Breathe slowly and deeply, go inside yourself and connect with your Inner Wisdom (sometimes called your Higher Self, your personal angels, your intuition, the Force, Spirit ...). Ask that part of you to lead you into a pathway of forgiving yourself and others that works for you.

Commit yourself to following your Inner Wisdom. If you truly wish to be free and you're willing to follow your own inner guidance, you can be free.

Now here's a practical tool called inventory work that has been very effective for me in the process of releasing shame and guilt. Remember that the goal is to clear away old guilt, shame, and resentment that may be blocking the flow of good into your life.

JOURNALING

Here's what you do: In your notebook or journal, write down *everything* about which you feel guilt, regret, embarrassment, or shame. Go back to your earliest memories and write down everything you can recall about which you feel any guilt. Just the facts will do. Depending on your particular history, it may be very important to write about any sexual behavior about which you feel guilty, embarrassed, or ashamed. In this culture, almost all of us need some healing of guilt and/or shame related to past sexual behavior. If this is true for you, just write it down along with other things.

This assignment may be completed in one sitting, over several days, or over several weeks or even months. The most important thing is to get your journal, get a pen, get honest, and get started. Once you've started, ideally, you'll write something on this assignment at least once a week or more often until it's completed.

Do whatever is necessary for you to feel at ease about keeping your writing safe and private. If you're concerned about others finding it and reading it, find a good hiding place or put it in a locked drawer, cabinet, or briefcase. Do what you need to do to neutralize any anxiety about your writing being discovered by those who might not respect it or by anyone who might be harmed by reading it.

As you write, you may at times be flooded or overwhelmed with feelings. If this should happen, pause for a moment, breathe deeply, remind yourself that these feelings are coming up to be released and healed, breathe some more, and continue. If tears come, let them flow. Tears are a gift for cleansing. Some wise anonymous person said, "What soap does for the body, tears do for the soul."

Breathe through and release any painful energy that comes to the surface as you write. The writing isn't causing the pain. The writing only brings the pain to the surface into your conscious awareness. The pain has been there for a long time. If it were going to kill you, you already would be dead! Feeling it and releasing it is part of healing.

Remember that pain isn't your enemy. If you allow it, pain can be your teacher and your motivator. Keep writing until you honestly feel complete. Congratulate yourself for putting all this down in writing.

MOVING FORWARD, GOING DEEPER

The next step of releasing guilt and forgiving yourself is to share what you've written with at least one other person. You can carefully choose the person you trust to be your listener. It may be a clergyperson, a therapist, a friend, or someone in "Twelve Step recovery" (Alcoholics Anonymous, Narcotics Anonymous, Overeaters Anonymous, and others) which teaches the importance of inventory work.

It's important that the listener be nonjudgmental and willing to commit to keeping the information confidential. Ideally, your listener will be a person who has completed a similar process in their own journey towards happiness and health. This also needs to be a person who is comfortable giving affirmation and support.

When you've finished writing this assignment, schedule a time to meet personally with your trusted listener. Allow plenty of time and create a setting where you won't be interrupted or distracted. Read your assignment to your listener, again remembering that any pain you experience in doing this is coming up to be released and healed. Keep breathing and keep reading until you're complete. If tears should come as your read, let them flow. They're washing away the toxic sludge.

As you review your writing assignment with your listener, look for people to whom you may need to make amends or restitution. Circle the names of those persons. (Probably the first person to whom you need to make amends is yourself.) Amends or restitution can take the form of a sincere apology, actual monetary payments, or regularly sending positive energy to the person until you feel free. Often, the most effective and meaningful amends are "living amends" (that is to say, changing the way you live in such a way that you are no longer harming yourself or others and, therefore, no longer feeling guilty).

When you're finished reading your assignment to your listener, ask your listener to give you some affirmation and support for your work. You may or may not choose to create a ritual with your listener to symbolize your letting go of the pain of the past. It can be as simple as burning pages of inventory work or having a pitcher of water and basin nearby where you can symbolically wash your hands.

MORE JOURNALING

Ask yourself, "What did I become aware of, learn or relearn by doing my inventory and reading it aloud? How do I feel now that it's complete?" Make notes in your journal about your feelings and about the lessons you learned or relearned from writing your inventory or reading it aloud. Share your answers with your accountability partner(s) and/or your trusted listener.

After discussing this with at least one other person, make a list in your journal of the persons to whom you owe amends or restitution. Beside each name, write down exactly what you will do to make amends/make restitution and write down a target date for taking the action. Be sure that any amends you make won't cause harm to yourself or to any other person.

Before actually making any amends, I strongly recommend that you discuss this list item by item with a spiritually mature person and ask for their feedback and guidance. Some people making amends without any guidance do too little and some do too much. Receiving guidance from a spiritually mature person can be extremely helpful. I am available for consultation on this or other subjects.

I know one person who refused to write or share an inventory. Without consulting anyone for guidance, this person thought that she would have to locate an ex-spouse after many years of no contact and make amends directly to the ex, something I personally would be very unlikely to recommend. Another person I know decided impulsively without any guidance that he needed to tell the spouse about all the times he had been sexually unfaithful in the marriage. Again, this is something that I personally wouldn't recommend in most cases.

Don't let your fear of making amends stop you from writing and sharing your inventory. You may find that a spiritually mature mentor would make the process of restitution much less difficult than you would make it yourself.

I am available to consult with readers through phone calls, email, or SKYPE about the whole process of releasing shame by doing inventory work and making restitution. However, I would encourage you to first consider any local mentors who are available and suitable.

Report regularly to an accountability partner (anyone to whom you choose to hold yourself accountable) how you're doing with making your amends by your target dates. It's okay to revise your target dates if you have unavoidable delays, but don't procrastinate unnecessarily. Work through the list with honest intention and effort. You'll be amazed at the good results.

CELEBRATE!

If you've had the courage and commitment to complete this step of your process, you deserve a reward and/or a celebration. *Plan and give yourself one!* It may or may not be something you buy for yourself. It may or may not cost money. Get quiet, go inside, and ask your Inner Wisdom, "What would be a fitting reward and celebration for this awesome healing work I'm doing?" Keep asking and listen for the answer. *Then do it!*

It may be a half-day or a full day off work to do nothing. It may be a beautiful certificate of achievement you create for yourself. It may be a phone call to someone special whose voice you haven't heard in a while. It may be a bouquet of your favorite flowers. Whatever it is, just be sure it's something that nurtures and affirms you.

The previous experience of doing inventory work is useful for healing guilt *and* shame. Most of us decide that if we've made mistakes or done some things about which we feel guilty, then we must be bad people and, subsequently, we feel ashamed. Sharing our regrets/guilt list with a nonjudgmental, supportive person and making amends helps us to release guilt and also helps us to see ourselves as human rather than bad (that is to say, it neutralizes toxic shame).

To further heal our toxic shame, we continue to affirm the truth about ourselves, knowing that we're spiritual beings on a human journey and that we're innately lovable, valuable, and precious. We *act as if* we believe that until we do! Other pieces of this process also help to address internalized shame issues. *Hang in there!*

CONSIDER PROFESSIONAL SUPPORT

It's important to note that healing toxic shame is an area of personal evolution that very often needs the attention of a skilled professional. Possibly some readers can begin and complete the process of shame releasing without professional assistance. *I would encourage any reader who does inventory work to seek professional consultation if the process becomes very painful or is in any way disruptive of normal functioning for more than a day or two.* This would be a very rare occurrence, but not outside the realm of possibility. If the reader doing inventory work is an active member of a stable, high functioning peer support group, this group can also be extremely helpful as you do your forgiveness work.

Again, remember that I'm available by appointment for consultation, *although I don't do crisis or emergency consultation. For crises or emergencies, I highly recommend that readers seek support from local resources in order to receive the best real-time, in-person emergency care with proper follow-up.* One resource that is almost always available is your local hospital emergency room. Most of them have health care professionals trained to intervene in mental health crises.

The next step of your forgiveness process is ...

FORGIVING OTHERS

First, know that *you have an absolute, inalienable right to be mad, sad, and/or hurt.* If anyone has ever abused you, cheated you, neglected you, abandoned you, lied to you, discriminated against you, ignored you, overlooked you, or hurt you or someone you love in any way, *you have a right to feel whatever you feel about that, absolutely and without any doubt whatsoever.*

In some circumstances, anger is a very reasonable and sane response. The energy of anger can be grounded and properly focused and channeled to create necessary positive change. Once the positive changes are made, however, the remaining anger energy can be harmlessly released. Anger held onto creates resentments that can poison a person's soul and absolutely destroy any chance of increasing that person's happiness and robust good health.

The good news is that no one has to carry old useless anger forever. Anger and resentment can be harmlessly released so that the energy of happiness and health can flow into that psychic space, healing any old hurts where the anger used to be. Again, in releasing anger and hurt (also known as forgiving) we *aren't* saying the hurtful thing that happened should have happened, or that it's okay that it happened, or that the injured person deserved to be hurt. In forgiving, one is simply saying, *"I'm willing to release the pain, the anger, the hurt, in order to allow greater happiness and health to flow into my life."*

Again, releasing old anger is typically a process, not an event. It may take time. If it does, no worries, no problem. Once begun with commitment and clear intention, forgiveness work tends to flow with its own momentum.

THE RULE OF 51%

Again, the 51% rule applies. When 51% of your resentments are released and healed, miracles will begin to happen in your life.

THE MAGIC OF FEELING YOUR FEELINGS

The "magic key" to releasing your anger is that it must first be felt and then expressed. Too often, we're told to forgive, but we're given no permission or support to fully feel and express our anger. I'm here to support you in feeling and expressing your anger and any other pain so that it can be harmlessly released.

JOURNALING

In your journal, make a list of everyone you can remember who has ever hurt or angered you. Write down their names and briefly what they did. Nothing is too big, too small, or too old to be included. Often, family members and others we may (or may not) cherish and love most, including parents, siblings, ex- or current spouses, in-laws, our children, and others will be at or near the top of the list if we're truly honest. Your list may include people who are now deceased.

Your list also may include groups of people or institutions. Maybe your list will include God. Write that down. Believe me, God can handle it. Maybe your list will include a disease or a natural disaster. Whoever or whatever angers or hurts you, put it on the list.

Some people say, "I'm not angry at anyone.... I've dealt with all that." I would gently ask that person, "Have you ever struggled with depression?" If so, I would encourage you to write down the things that you find to be depressing. Some wise person said, "Depression is frozen anger...." It may be that underneath your depression is anger that needs to be brought to the surface to be neutralized and released.

Also, if you believe you have no anger toward anyone or anything, can you sincerely bless that person or thing and wish them nothing but good? If you cannot, you most likely have some residual anger to release.

As you write about your anger, breathe and release. If tears come, let them flow. There's no need to be afraid of any painful feelings that may come to the surface as you write. If these feelings were powerful enough to kill you, you would already be dead. Breathe and release and write. Keep writing until you honestly feel complete.

When you've finished your list, go back through it and underline or circle five or six names/items that seem to have the most emotional charge for you. Choose one of the names/entities.

In your journal, date and begin to write an honest letter to that person/institution/entity. Don't edit, judge, or censor the letter in any way, as you won't be sending it, and no one will grade it for spelling errors. Let your feelings pour out onto the paper. Use profanity if it comes to mind. Someone said, "Profanity is the poetry of anger and we all need poetry." Be thorough in describing everything that the person/entity did that angers you.

Again, breathe and release as you write. If you find yourself feeling very angry, GREAT! The anger has always been there, often just below and outside of your conscious awareness. As you become aware of it, you can release it.

Have a dry bath towel close by. If you wish, you can pick up the bath towel and start wringing it into knots, voicing your anger as you do so. Punch a pillow if you need to do so. If you feel like screaming, scream into a pillow. This will help release the anger without alarming the neighbors!

Another great technique is to take ice cubes out to the sidewalk or to the asphalt patio. Hurling the ice cubes and watching them shatter can be an excellent release, as effective as breaking dishes, except this is even better because there's no mess to clean up afterward. The ice melts and the water evaporates.

Taking a brisk walk also can help to release repressed anger energy if you begin the walk with the conscious intention of releasing anger as you go. As you walk, stomp, and pound the pavement, breathe deeply, and blow out anger through your mouth and nostrils. Repeat as often as necessary.

Some of this may seem weird or silly. Who's watching? Some readers are thinking, *What if I lose control and go crazy?* Not a chance. If you were going to lose control or go crazy you would have done so long ago. Your Inner Wisdom has protected and preserved you and will continue to do so.

Continue your writing, taking whatever breaks you need to release old anger energy that comes to the surface. After thoroughly reviewing the things that the person/entity has done to hurt or anger you and thoroughly expressing ALL of your feelings about that, finish the letter with something like this *if and only if you're ready to do so*:

"I'm no longer willing to give you power in my life. I refuse to be your victim. I'm no longer willing to carry hurt and anger (or depression) because of what you did. I survived you. I release you to your highest good. I forgive you. I bless you. Your actions have no more power in my life."

If you aren't willing to take the final releasing step just above to totally release those who have hurt or angered you, complete the following statement and add it to the letter:

"I'm not yet willing to release you. For now, I continue to be your victim. For now, I'll continue to give you power to damage and diminish my health, my happiness, my life, and my power to make a positive difference in the world. I'll continue to carry my anger and hurt for at least another _____ (specific period of time – hours, days, weeks, months or years)." Then end the letter in the way that feels appropriate.

If you didn't reach the point of releasing, continue to write at least one honest letter a week to this person/entity until you're willing to completely release.

GOING FORWARD, GOING DEEPER

Schedule time with a trusted listener. Share the letter with your listener. You can share two or more letters with your trusted listener on the same date if you choose. Ask your listener for affirmation and support for the work you're doing. If you wish, create a simple (or elaborate) ritual to symbolize your new freedom.

Continue writing and sharing with your listener until you've written letters to at least five of the people on your list of people who have hurt and/or angered you. Be sure these are the people who have hurt or angered you the *most*.

If at any time during this process, you think that having the support of a professional therapist or other professional caregiver would be helpful to you, get it. This is deep, transformative work. In our culture, the professionals who witness and support transformative work are most often mental health professionals or specially trained clergy.

I am available to witness and support this work if requested. I also support you in seeking services from a qualified local provider. Just be sure that if you seek the support of a local professional caregiver that the chosen caregiver is comfortable facilitating anger and shame release work.

Also, be sure that they've done their own anger and shame release work. This is a qualification not shared by all mental health professionals. Some professionals use the motto, "I just sell this stuff (mental health). I don't buy it."

FOLLOW YOUR INNER GUIDANCE

If you write letters to the five or six people who have been most hurtful or anger-provoking in your life and share those letters with a trusted listener, you will then have the skills, strength, insight, and maturity to continue and complete your forgiveness work. If you need to write more letters, you'll know how to do that. Go inside and ask your Inner Wisdom for guidance. When you receive the guidance, follow it.

By the way, this letter-writing process also is very helpful in resolving grief issues. If you've had significant losses in your life, writing letters and reading them to a trusted listener can help you move through the grief process to acceptance and serenity.... More about this in my next book!

CELEBRATE!

If you've given this work your best effort, it's time to create another celebration and/or give yourself another reward. Go inside and ask your Inner Wisdom for guidance in creating your reward/celebration. *Then do it!*

BONUS AT NO EXTRA COST

As a bonus I have one more forgiveness tool to share with you. This comes directly from Twelve-step Recovery literature, specifically the *"Big Book"* of Alcoholics Anonymous. Page 552 of the *"Big Book"* suggests:

"If you have a resentment you want to be free of, if you will pray for the person or the thing that you resent, you will be free. If you will ask in prayer for everything you want for yourself to be given to them, you will be free. Ask for their health, their prosperity, their happiness, and you will be free. Even when you don't really want it for them, and your prayers are only words and you don't mean it, go ahead and do it anyway. Do it every day for two weeks and you will find you have come to mean it and to want it for them. You will realize that where you used to feel bitterness and resentment and hatred, you now feel compassionate understanding and love."

I have used this prayer with excellent results and I highly recommend it. It works very well along with the other tools recommended in this chapter. Even if you don't believe in prayer, you can visualize the person, institution, or entity on your anger list and send positive energy and good will. See the listed person or entity surrounded by white light and filled with the white light of divine blessing or good will until the negative energy is completely neutralized.

YOU ARE ONE IN ONE THOUSAND

If you've chosen to do forgiveness work as suggested, you can count yourself among those who are truly exceptional students and dedicated seekers of Truth and Light. It's estimated that approximately one in one thousand people (.1%) in modern Western industrialized culture are willing to undertake personal evolution work requiring such focus, honesty, commitment, and perseverance as inventory work.

SELF-EMPOWERMENT WHILE MAKING A DIFFERENCE

Hopefully, by this point in our process, you've begun to experience forgiveness as a self-empowerment process. Remember, forgiveness is about taking back the power to create the life you want and deserve, a life overflowing with happiness and robust good health.

As you proceed through your process of forgiving self and others, your individual consciousness will rise higher and higher and you'll be helping to elevate the collective consciousness. Being free of guilt, shame, and resentment will bring a degree of internal peace otherwise not attainable. Also, creating within yourself this degree of peace will have a positive influence on every significant relationship in your life. Your peace will be contagious as you live the prayer, "Let there be peace on earth, and let it begin with me...."

Chapter 7

"BE THE CHANGE YOU WISH
TO SEE IN THE WORLD"

THE QUOTE ABOVE IS ATTRIBUTED TO MAHATMA GANDHI, who is widely recognized as one of the world's greatest spiritual and political leaders of the twentieth century. His wisdom is simple yet profound.

With mass media news reporting being as sensational and violent as it has become, many of us slide into despair about the state of the world and become hopeless about an individual's power to make any noticeable difference. Others self-medicate with a combination of mood and mind-altering substances and compulsive escapist behaviors (for example, compulsive exercise, shopping, gambling, sex, work, hoarding, toxic religion, overeating and others) in order to distract themselves from despair, hopelessness, and depression. I offer you another option.

Fill in the blank in this statement: I wish the whole world were more _____. Whatever you wish for, you can make the whole world more like that by first making yourself more like that and become happier and healthier in body/mind/spirit in the process.

Suppose, for example, you wish the world as a whole were kinder. You can make the world kinder by making a serious commitment to kindness then consciously and conscientiously practicing kindness to the best of your ability daily.

THE JOY OF COMPANIONSHIP

For this to be meaningful and successful, I highly recommend recruiting at least one "playmate" if you have not already done so who will also fill in the blank and make a commitment to being the change. You and your playmate/accountability partner can hold yourselves accountable to one another in any fashion that works for you. For ideas on how to be a good accountability partner, you might review the suggestions in the Introduction.

THE RULE OF 51%

Once again, you do not have to achieve anything near perfection in your practice of "being the change." When 51% of your waking energy on average is devoted to "being the change you wish to see in the world," great and wonderful changes will occur within you *and* within the world as you experience it.

Some people try to change the outer world while their inner worlds (their hearts, minds, soul, spirit, "guts") are dominated by anger, desperation, fear, grief, guilt, and/or shame. Efforts to change the world while struggling either consciously or unconsciously with such inner turmoil are doomed to failure.

In order to change the world, we must first rediscover our inner core of pure love, light, and joy. Once we rediscover that energy within ourselves and allow it to flow through us to others, we're truly changing the world in which we live.

Health and happiness are contagious! (Unfortunately, so are toxicity and misery, but we won't dwell on that.) To the extent that you become the change you want to see in the world, you raise the collective vibration of the planet. Never doubt that your positive intentions and sincere efforts make a world of difference.

Consider that your positive intentions and sincere efforts at being the change may never be featured on the twenty-four-hour commercial news cycle or make the headlines of *USA Today* or even your hometown weekly. Yet your efforts and the positive efforts of countless others are collectively neutralizing and transforming the lower, slower, darker energies circulating around the planet. Otherwise, the human race would have completely self-destructed long ago.

JOURNALING

Turn to a new page in your journal and write at the top of the page:

I wish the whole world were more _____.

Then quickly start writing a list of descriptive words to fill in the blank. Do not edit, censor, or judge what you have written. Just keep writing descriptive words until your list feels complete.

Go back through the list and pick out one describer that seems most important and appealing to you. Circle that word. Now begin to list specific ways you can "be that change" in your world. Let your imagination flow. Writing these ideas on the list doesn't obligate you to anything. Just imagine and write. It's okay to ask your accountability partner(s) or others you trust to help you brainstorm this list. Asking for help creating this list could lead to some fascinating and enlightening conversations!

Once you have a list of ideas about how you can begin to be that change, choose one or more specific actions and *get busy*. Set target dates to complete specific action.

Makes notes in your journal about your experiences with being the change. Be sure to note what you are learning or relearning in this process. Share those notes with your accountability partner(s).

MAKING A DIFFERENCE FOR ALL HUMANKIND

Meanwhile, always remember that for today, higher/brighter/lighter energies (that is to say, the energy of love, compassion, kindness, empathy, acceptance, forgiveness, joy, and others) are elevating the collective consciousness of the human family and all is well. Your sincere and intentional efforts at being the change will raise your individual level of consciousness and will be an ongoing inspiration to others. The positive ripple effect is infinite as we rejoice in the fact that we're living to see the sun rise again with another opportunity to move step by step in a positive direction.

Chapter 8

KEEP AND CULTIVATE YOUR
SENSE OF HUMOR

THE MOST MODERN, SCIENTIFICALLY RIGOROUS RESEARCH
confirms what has been known for millennia; that is people who
enjoy and generate humor are happier and healthier than those
who don't. Ancient Hebrew scripture observes, "A happy heart is
good medicine and a cheerful mind works healing..." (Proverbs
17:22, *Old Testament*).

Laughter is our birthright. It's innate and as natural as
breathing. Infants begin smiling during the first few weeks of life
and laugh out loud within the first few months.

Numerous research studies in modern times have
documented the measurable positive influence of humor on
physical, emotional, cognitive, social, and spiritual health.
Benefits have been reported in geriatrics, oncology, critical care,
pain management, psychiatry, rehabilitation, rheumatology,
home care, palliative care, hospice care, terminal care, and
general patient care. A quick on-line search reveals plentiful
details. This chapter summarizes relevant findings of current
research into the mind/body/spirit health value of laughter and
offers suggestions for readers who decide to use humor to
improve the quality of their own lives and make a difference for
humankind while doing so.

DR. FRY'S PIONEERING RESEARCH

An early pioneer in the study of the health benefits of humor, Dr. William Fry, Jr., M.D., called laughter "inner jogging." Dr. Fry's research over a period of fifty years showed that laughter enhances respiration and circulation; oxygenates the blood; increases alertness, creativity, and memory; suppresses stress-related hormones in the brain; and activates the immune system. It helps the one who laughs think more clearly while enhancing cardiovascular flexibility, developing abdominal muscles, speeding up metabolism, and burning extra calories. Later research confirmed that laughing for ten to fifteen minutes per day can burn approximately forty calories, which could be enough to reduce weight by three or four pounds over the course of a year.

DR. NORMAN COUSINS

... was another pioneer in the study of the therapeutic value of humor. In 1964, he was diagnosed with ankylosing spondylitis, a crippling degenerative disease with inflammation of the spine and large joints. The condition left him in almost constant pain. His doctor said he would die within a few months. Dr. Cousins disagreed and theorized that positive emotions would help him feel better.

With his doctor's consent, he checked himself out of the hospital and checked himself into a nearby hotel so he could have quick access to medical monitoring and emergency care if needed. He began watching a continuous stream of classic comedy films and similar "laughing matter." He later said, "I made the joyous discovery that ten minutes of belly rippling laughter would give me at least two hours of pain-free sleep when nothing else would, not even morphine."

His condition steadily improved. Within six months, he was back on his feet, and within two years, he was able to return to his full-time job. His 1979 book about his experience, *An Anatomy of an Illness as Perceived by the Patient – Reflections on Healing and Regeneration,* is a classic and was made into a movie. He helped to establish a humor task force at UCLA medical school to support studies on laughter and healing. One of his more well-known quotes is, "He who laughs, LASTS!"

OTHER RESEARCHERS

Another prominent humor researcher, Dr. Lee Berk, Professor of Medicine, Loma Linda University, found that even anticipating a funny event can be good for your health. In one study, he told half of a research group that in three days they would be treated to a video of Gallagher, a well-known comic at that time. Blood tests showed that those who were given this information experienced a drop in stress hormones and an increase in chemicals that strengthen the immune system. Changes got more and more pronounced as the test subjects got closer to show time!

Dr. Berk stated, "For the most part, when you go and get medical treatment, a clinician is not necessarily going to tell you to take two aspirins and watch Laurel and Hardy, but the reality is that's where we are and it's more real than ever. There's a real science to this. And it's as real as taking a drug."

A new branch of medicine called psychoneuroimmunology studies and seeks to maximize the positive interaction between the brain, the endocrine system, and the immune system. Research in this field is showing, for example, that positive feelings can stimulate the spleen, producing an increase in red blood cells and a corresponding increase in the number of cancer-fighting cells. These cells can destroy cancer cells one by one, leaving normal tissue untouched (unlike chemotherapy which cannot distinguish between normal and malignant cells).

A study in Norway found that people with a strong sense of

humor outlived those who didn't laugh as much. The difference was particularly notable for those battling cancer.

Other researchers have found evidence that humor can alleviate allergy symptoms, increase pain tolerance, reduce the risk of stroke and heart attack, and even help diabetics control their blood sugar. One study found that people with heart disease are 40% less likely to see the humor in life's everyday absurdities than were people the same age with healthy hearts.

RX FOR HEALTHIER RELATIONSHIPS

Humor and laughter can be an enhancement to personal relationships with romantic partners, friends and family, or co-workers. These relationships, to a great extent, determine the quality of our lives. Shared laughter is a great tool for keeping relationships fresh and interesting, adding joy, vitality, and resilience to the mix of emotions generated in human relationships. Humor applied wisely improves morale and promotes group bonding and teamwork.

When we laugh with one another, a positive bond is created which helps to neutralize conflict and anger between people. Humor can also help to heal disagreements and hurts and build bridges during difficult times. It can help those struggling in relationships to forget resentments, judgments, criticisms, and doubt. We can use humor to lower everyone's stress level and communicate in a way that strengthens the relationship rather than tears it down.

THE A.T. &.T. TEST

Like any powerful tool, humor can be used for great good or can be misused to cause damage. Before injecting humor into a situation, always use the "A. T. & T. test": Is it Appropriate? Is it Timely? Is it Tasteful? If you can answer "yes" to all three questions, it's a "GO."

To improve relationships, use humor *always* as a tool, *never* as a weapon. Laugh *with* others, not at their expense. Laughing *with* others builds confidence, brings people together, and pokes fun at our common dilemmas. Laughing *at* others destroys confidence, ruptures teamwork, and victimizes individuals or groups as the "butt of the joke."

Many renowned spiritual teachers and theologians consider humor and laughter important spiritual practices (for examples, see https://tinyurl.com/yar4zsmj)

FAMOUS HUMORISTS

Humor helps you keep a positive, optimistic outlook through difficult situations, disappointments, and loss. More than just a reprieve from sadness and pain, laughter can give you the courage and strength to find new sources of meaning and inspiration. Anne Lamott, an American author, public speaker, and writing teacher, said, "Laughter is carbonated holiness."

HUMOR AND HOPE

Humor inspires hope. Tina Clark, author of *Southern Discomfort* and other popular works, wrote "Laughter is the tangible evidence of hope." Over the past several decades, repeated studies have reported an apparent connection between health outcomes and states of hope.

Many historians have documented that Abraham Lincoln had an extraordinary sense of humor (for more information, see http://www.mrlincolnandfriends.org/humor-and-personality/) According to his contemporaries, he always loved telling and listening to funny stories. He also relished jokes and pranks. Some say it was his greatest coping mechanism and survival skill.

Lincoln's life was darkened many times by tragedy and grief, disappointments and defeats, both politically and personally. However, he never lost his well-developed sense of humor.

Lincoln's mother, younger brother, and older sister all died when he was a child. He was estranged from his father, who died without seeing his grandchildren. The love of his young adult life, whom he intended to marry, suddenly became ill and died.

He seemed to personally grieve the injury or death of every Civil War soldier on both sides of the conflict. In 1862, in the midst of the horrible war, his twelve-year-old son Willie died of typhoid fever. Later that same year, one of his dearest friends died in battle. President Lincoln wrote a deeply sensitive and eloquent condolence letter to his fallen friend's daughter. Without using the word, he nevertheless described eloquently the power of hope when he wrote:

"In this sad world of ours, sorrow comes to all; and...with bitterest agony. Perfect relief is not possible, except with time. You cannot now realize that you will ever feel better. Is not this so? And yet it is a mistake. You are sure to be happy again. To know this, which is certainly true, will make you some less miserable now. I have had experience enough to know what I say; and you need only to believe it, to feel better at once."

GRIEVING OUR WAY INTO HAPPINESS

Paradoxically, one way to enjoy humor more is to allow oneself to grieve. Again, ancient Hebrew wisdom astutely instructs: "To everything there is a season, and a time to every purpose under the heaven...A time to weep, and a time to laugh; a time to mourn, and a time to dance ..." (Ecclesiastes 3:1, 3:4, *the Bible*).

Those who refuse to mindfully grieve their losses find their capacity to enjoy humor and life in general to be greatly inhibited. Unfortunately, the culture of the industrialized Western world, including the United States, perpetuates many misconceptions and taboos around grief. This makes it difficult if not impossible for most people to progress through the integration and healing of loss.

To effectively grieve so that one may experience inner peace and true joy may require the companionship and guidance of a professional grief mentor (sometimes called a grief counselor). Readers with significant unresolved grief could benefit mightily from the services of a grief professional. Once the grief is integrated, processed, and released, then humor and life in general are much easier to enjoy.

I have a great passion for grief mentoring and am available for one-to-one, family, or small group consultation. I have been presenting grief education workshops to professionals and to community groups for many years. If you're interested in arranging for me to visit your area to provide community education and/or a retreat, please see my contact information at the end of the book.

Even in the midst of resolving grief, laughter and humor can help to soften the sharpness of emotional pain. The great Irish playwright and Nobel Prize winner, George Bernard Shaw, observed, "Life does not cease to be funny when someone dies any more than it ceases to be serious when someone laughs."

I accompanied a grieving widow and her adult daughter to make burial arrangements for their just deceased husband and father. While appropriately sad, their grief was mitigated by their faith. The daughter even joked, "I want a sign by the casket which reads, 'This is only the shell. The nut has gone to heaven.'"

ACTION STEPS

Readers who wish to add more humor to your lives may play with any or all of the following suggestions:

- Notice what makes you laugh (for example: slapstick, Three Stooges, stand up, romantic comedy movies, classic TV sitcoms) and intentionally seek it regularly. Enjoy it fully.
- Smile more often. Smiling generally precedes laughter

and sets a positive tone for interaction with others. Like laughter, smiling is contagious. At any time, whether alone or with others, practice smiling – and notice the effect on yourself and others. Victor Borge, popular comedian and ventriloquist from an earlier era said, "A smile is the shortest distance between two people."

- Start your own collection of recorded humor (audio recordings or video recordings). Keep a file of funny jokes, cartoons, and stories and refer to it often. When you hear or see something funny, capture it and add it to the file.
- Display funny sayings, quotes, posters, pet pictures, snapshots, and cartoons where you'll see them daily.
- Laugh at yourself. Don't take yourself too seriously. Embrace your imperfections. Redeem personal blunders by turning them into funny stories. Tell funny stories about yourself when appropriate. An unknown wise person said, "Blessed are those who can laugh at themselves. They will never cease to be amused."
- Whenever you have a decision to laugh or not to laugh, choose to laugh. Certainly, at times, laughter is clearly inappropriate, but most of life is neither very sad nor very delightful unless we make it so. Laughing can make it more delightful. One anonymous wise person said, "We'll laugh at this one day. Why not now?"
- Give yourself permission to be more childlike. Toddlers typically laugh once every five minutes or about four hundred times per day. Adults generally laugh fifteen times per day or less.
- Schedule and spend time with people who laugh easily at themselves and at life's absurdities. Their attitude is contagious. When they tell a joke or funny story,

laugh out loud, even if you don't think it's funny. Both you and the other person will feel better immediately, and the laughter will draw you closer together. Every comedian appreciates an audience.

- Avoid social isolation. Balance healthy solitude and reflection with positive pleasant time enjoying the company of others. Research has documented that people are thirty times more likely to laugh in social settings than in solitude.
- Find and participate in a laughter yoga (Hasya yoga) class.
- Enjoy the humor section of your public library or bookstore.
- Read the comics section of the newspaper.
- Rescue a kitten or puppy or even a middle-aged pet. My two four-legged middle-aged fur babies make me laugh out loud every day.
- Organize one or more group outings to a comedy club.
- Host a game night with friends and make it clear that the goal is to have fun. Make it clear that the "Grand Prize Winner" for the evening is the person who laughs the most and has the most fun, whatever the score at the end of the game might be.
- Ask people, "What's the funniest thing that happened to you today? This week? In your life?" Some will remember something and share it with you. Having a good laugh together will be a positive bond in your relationship. Don't be disappointed or judgmental if they can't think of anything on the spot. Asking them the question may stimulate them to reflect and eventually remember something funny. Their memory of a humorous event will brighten their day and help raise the collective consciousness, whether or not they ever share that memory with you. Just keep

asking and notice the responses you get and the feelings generated when you do share a good laugh.

• Take the "Humor Habit Pledge":

> *I don't want to live my life crabby.*
> *I'd rather be healthy and happy.*
> *So, I pledge I'll find humor around me.*
> *I'll make sure fun people surround me.*
> *When there's a humorous chance, I must grab it*
> *So I can develop my own Humor Habit!*

STRONG MEDICINE

It's true that laughter really is strong medicine. The ability to laugh, play, and have fun not only makes life more enjoyable but also helps you to solve problems, connect with others, and think more creatively. The willingness to laugh easily and often is a huge asset for problem-solving, enhancing relationships, and improving physical, emotional, cognitive, social, and spiritual health. Even better – this priceless medicine is fun, free, and easy to use.

MAKING A DIFFERENCE

As you intentionally integrate humor, laughter, and play more and more into your life, new opportunities for laughing with friends, coworkers, acquaintances, and loved ones will develop. You'll raise your own individual consciousness as you view yourself and others from a more relaxed, positive, and joyful perspective. At the same time, you'll be contributing higher, brighter, lighter energy to the collective consciousness and bringing good to the entire human family.

IN WRITING this chapter I enjoyed the following resources:

Help Guide: Your Trusted Guide to Mental Health and Wellness
Helpguide.org/articles/mental-
health/laughteristhebestmedicine.htm

LAUGHTER ONLINE UNIVERSITY
www.laughteronlineuniversity.com

Chapter 9

ACKNOWLEDGE AND
EMBRACE YOUR MORTALITY
AND YOUR IMMORTALITY

BELOVED READER, YOU MAY NOT APPRECIATE THE FOLLOWING
gentle reminder: *None of us gets out of here alive. We are all going
to die.*

OPTING OUT OF CULTURAL NONSENSE – AGAIN!

Acknowledging the universality of physical death flies in the face
of death denial, death defiance, and death avoidance, all of which
have pervaded western industrialized culture for centuries. Some
astute European observer quipped, "Americans think that death
is optional." Death denial/ defiance/avoidance is so complete for
some people that it often remains intact until the very last
breath.

In Western industrialized culture, children learn from the
cradle forward that death is a topic to avoid thinking or talking
about. Discussing or even acknowledging death is
uncomfortable. If you doubt this, read the Sunday obituaries in
your local newspaper or on-line. The euphemisms substituted
for the words "died" are amazingly creative and diverse.

Also, if you doubt that you personally have been affected by
our cultural taboos around acknowledging death, notice how

comfortable or uncomfortable you are when referring to deceased persons in conversation using the words "death" or "died" or "dead." Just notice. Finally, if you doubt that you have internalized our cultural denial and avoidance of death, notice how resistant you are to read and/or complete the action steps and journaling suggestions included in this chapter.

Many people fear acknowledging death because they have never decided what they believe about the afterlife or they fear eternal damnation and punishment for being anything less than perfect. This is an unfortunate legacy of western Judeo-Christian religious teaching. This erroneous, shame-fear-and-guilt-based interpretation of the teaching of Jesus the Christ is so embedded in our cultural consciousness that even people who have never been particularly religious are negatively impacted by it.

FEAR OF FEELINGS

Another reason people avoid all things related to death is that this is an emotionally charged subject. Typical citizens of modern industrialized countries are pathetically inept at appropriately expressing or effectively processing intense emotions. Culturally, we value logic, reason, rationality, and control (considered masculine traits) while we devalue feelings and intuition (considered "effeminate" or "womanish" or "sissified" and therefore inferior). Unless the feelings are related to competitive sports events or expressed in popular music, intense emotions are considered a weakness and a loss of control. This is an unfortunate legacy of centuries of oppressive patriarchy predominant in many cultures worldwide up until this very day.

One exception to this is that privileged males are allowed to feel and express intense anger with impunity. However, expression of any other intense emotion by a male, no matter how privileged he may be, automatically and instantly makes him a weak "girly man."

Avoiding emotionally charged subjects may bring some temporary escape from discomfort, but the cost is high in the long term. The more a subject is avoided, the more frightening it becomes. The subject of one's own death and/or that of others sooner or later has to be addressed.

THE COST OF DEATH DENIAL

Those who continue to avoid and deny death reach the end of life totally unprepared financially, emotionally, and spiritually for the next step of the journey. By avoiding the reality of death and other emotionally charged subjects, they rob themselves and others of enjoying each precious day. Sadly, many die having never fully lived.

If living stretches into infinity, or if we fool ourselves into pretending so, then living is really nothing special (day in ... day out ... ho hum....) If we truly accept and believe that our lifetimes on this earth and the lives of our loved ones are temporary, then every single day becomes a priceless gift to be treasured and enjoyed to the fullest. *Carpe diem!*

Knowing that any day – any moment - could be the last for any of us, we are more likely to make peace within ourselves and with others. We are more likely to say the important things we need to say, like "I love you," "Thank you," "I'm sorry, please forgive me," or "I forgive you." We are more likely to make peace with the Divine, or alternatively, to make peace with the idea that there is no Divinity. Either way, we are at peace. *Peace is a good thing.*

ANOTHER BIT OF MY PERSONAL STORY

In 1984, I was an emotionally and spiritually immature thirty-year-old. I was just out of a sudden unexpected divorce and unexpectedly and suddenly unemployed. My beautiful vibrant fifty-six-year-old mother was suddenly killed in an automobile accident. She had left my home two days earlier. I spoke with her two times by phone on the day she died. She was here, then she wasn't.

Two-and-one-half years later, before I was fully recovered from my divorce and my mother's death, my handsome blue-eyed fifty-eight-year-old father dropped dead of a heart attack. He left a beautiful corpse.

To my knowledge, neither of my parents had ever discussed with anyone matters such as whether they wanted a full body burial or a cremation and where they would want their remains to be placed. Neither of my parents had prepared a will or made any plans or arrangements for the distribution of their estates.

My siblings and I were at the mercy of our stepfather when our mother died and at the mercy of our stepmother when our father died. Surprisingly, neither my stepfather nor my stepmother were inclined to kindness, fairness, or sensitivity when it came to settling our parents' estates. It took literally twenty years to arbitrate my father's meager holdings. The sudden deaths of both my parents at relatively young ages have given me a sensitivity to and an awareness of the reality of death and the necessity of planning for it.

IS DEATH REALLY SUCH A BAD THING?

The inevitability of death is called bad by some (and therefore to be avoided) in that it means our time on this level of existence is limited. Most judge that to be a bad thing. Our physical bodies age, decline and sooner or later cease to function sufficiently for us to continue to live life as we know it in the human body. We draw our last breath, the soul is set free, and the body sooner or later decomposes, depending on how much embalming fluid is applied.

Most people in modern industrialized culture would say this is bad, but is it? Consider for a moment, would you truly want to live in this dimension in the same body for all eternity? Is it truly such a bad thing for the soul to be set free from the earthly body? Even if you could periodically trade in your physical body for a new one (like trading vehicles), would you really want to continue in this earthly mode forever and ever ...? *REALLY?*

For years, I have subscribed to the e-newsletter of Dr. Ben Kim, a wise young Korean health educator. I lifted the following from a recent newsletter of Dr. Kim's and filed it under "things that make you go hmmmmmmmm..."

> *"I'll tell you a secret. Something they don't teach you in your temple. The Gods envy us. They envy us because we're mortal, because any moment might be our last. Everything is more beautiful because we're doomed. You will never be lovelier than you are now. We will never be here again."*

> - Achilles (David Benioff, Troy)

Consider the following, written by Sarah Francati of St. John Fisher College in 2017:

"Our denial and distancing of death ultimately only harms us. Death should be more so looked at as a motivating force for life. ...if we turn the tables on the way we view death we can transition into seeing it as a peaceful process that brings us to eternal happiness and comfort. The first step in facing our denial is to come to terms with the fact that death is inevitable. We either can choose to shun away and distance ourselves, only making matters worse, or accept and embrace the process.... We need to distance ourselves from the feelings of fear and instead become more intimate with death. When we can accept that we are afraid, we need to embrace it then understand why we are and only then can we unravel acceptance. Ultimately (acceptance) rests in our desire to want to understand what death can offer us and accept the fact greater things potentially await us beyond the living world. We need to stop taking steps backwards from facing death and instead indulge in its mysteries and wonders. Only then can we move past our denial and embrace the beauty acceptance has to offer."

Sarah's complete statement is found at https://tinyurl.com/ya9vhhtf

YIN AND YANG

In contrast to death denial/defiance/avoidance, research has indicated that the Asian yin and yang philosophy of death – where life can't exist without death – allows individuals to use death as a reminder to enjoy life.

The eloquent Persian poet Kahlil Gibran wrote:

> *You would know the secret of death.*
> *But how shall you find it unless you seek it in the heart of*
>   *life? ...*
> *For life and death are one, even as the river and the sea*
>   *are one. ...*
> *...what is it to cease breathing, but to free the breath from*
>   *its restless tides,*
> *that it may rise and expand and seek God unencumbered?*
> *Only when you drink from the river of silence shall you*
>   *indeed sing.*
> *And when you have reached the mountain top, then you*
>   *shall begin to climb.*
> *And when the earth shall claim your limbs, then shall*
>   *you truly dance."*

This perspective assumes an afterlife and assumes that the afterlife is positive. Debates and theories about the afterlife, the hereafter, heaven and hell, nirvana, paradise, enlightenment and other related ideas echo through the centuries since the dawn of recorded time. I do not debate anything with anyone.

The bottom line for me is this: I am happier and therefore healthier believing that there is a reality beyond this present experience and that the reality beyond this life is a good place for *every* spiritual being on a human journey. (This belief is a tenet of Christian Universalism and other philosophies) I say, "If believing this makes me happier and healthier until this life ends, what is the harm in believing it?"

Here is one of my favorite passages from the Greek scriptures (often called the New Testament) about these topics:

> *"For this perishable (part of us) must put on the imperishable (nature), and this mortal (part of us, this nature that is capable of dying) must put on immortality (freedom from death). And when this perishable puts on the imperishable and this that was capable of dying puts on freedom from death, then shall be fulfilled the Scripture that says, Death is swallowed up (utterly vanquished forever) in and unto victory. O death, where is your victory? O death, where is your sting? ... thanks be to God, Who gives us the victory (making us conquerors)..."*

-I Corinthians 15:53-57 (Amplified Bible)

I have studied the entire Bible with an open heart and mind since childhood. I am aware of scriptures that are used to preach "hellfire and brimstone" in the hereafter. There are many interpretations to such scriptures. I choose where I place my focus. *My faith rests with a merciful and loving Creator.*

Beloved reader, know that *I support you one hundred per cent without condition* whatever you choose to believe about these matters. My only wish is that you mindfully choose thoughts, ideas, and beliefs that bring you peace.

ACTION STEPS

I offer these very specific, very gentle suggestions to assist you in accepting and even embracing the inevitability of death:

1. Discuss with a trusted family member or friend *other than your next of kin* how you would like your final arrangements to be handled if you died suddenly within the next day or two. The person you speak with is ideally a good listener who doesn't judge or give advice. Discussing final arrangements will make the reality of death clearer to you. When you begin this conversation you may not know exactly how you would like every detail to be managed. *Just begin the conversation.* Talking through these matters with someone you trust will help you decide.

2. Speak to your next of kin about these matters AFTER you have "practiced" with a different friend or family member. An excellent resource for those courageous and loving enough to initiate this conversation is The Conversation Project (https:// theconversationproject.org/). If your next of kin is very resistant to discussing these matters, let it drop temporarily but raise the issue again at another time, preferably when there are no distractions and no other pressing matters. Let your next of kin know that you will continue to initiate the discussion until some clear understanding is reached. Move ahead with your preparations whether or not your next of kin is willing to collaborate.

3. Make an appointment and consult with one or more

reputable funeral services professionals. Be an informed consumer. Learn about the legalities and the costs of various options. Finalize plans for the disposal of your body when you die. (The environmentalist in me insists that I encourage you to explore the option of a green burial.)

4. Finalize plans for the funeral, memorial service, "home going" or celebration of life you would prefer for yourself. Good news here is that there is truly no more a "rule book" to follow when it comes to planning this occasion. It can be as unique as your fingerprint. It can be very simple and very inexpensive or very elaborate and costly. If you want it to be very elaborate and costly, be sure to set aside enough money to cover the cost of the arrangements without creating a financial hardship for your survivors. Many people today leave firm commands that there be no funeral or memorial services of any kind, usually because their only experiences with end-of-life gatherings have been negative and awkward. Consider the possibility that a properly planned and prepaid gathering could be a great comfort for your survivors. I highly recommend the book *Creating Meaningful Funeral Experiences: A Guide for Families*, by Dr. Alan Wolfelt, available at www.centerforloss.com .

5. Seek competent legal assistance to prepare a will. Finalize it, knowing that it can be changed/updated/revised as you wish.

6. Prepare advance directives for the possibility that you could be mentally or physically incapacitated before your death. Your local hospice can help with this.

7. Consider writing down personal messages that you would want your dearest family and friends to have in the event of your death. Leave them where you know

they will be found or leave them with a trusted friend or relative.

8. Find and attend a Death Café. Search https://deathcafe.com/what *OR* https://www.facebook. com/deathcafe/ If you cannot find one within driving distance, consider hosting one.

JOURNALING

1. Visit http://wisdomquotes.com/death-quotes/ Scan through the quotes about death. When you find one that seems particularly meaningful, write it in your journal and then write down your responses to it. It would be optional to share your reflections with a trusted friend or family member.

2. Go back to *Chapter 5: Celebrate Your Spirituality* and review the list of Big Questions contained in that chapter. If you have not already found satisfactory answers for yourself, spend some time and energy pondering, reading, journaling, and/or talking with trusted friends or family about these questions. Find answers that bring you peace.

3. Make a "bucket list" of things you want to be sure to do before you die. Give each item a priority number and a target date. Get busy planning for the item at the top of the priority list.

4. Ask yourself the question, "How do I want people to remember me after I have died?" Write down your answer(s). Begin immediately to live in a way that you will be remembered as you wish to be remembered.

GETTING REAL WITH YOURSELF AND OTHERS

Following these suggestions will shatter your death denial/avoidance/defiance and neutralize your fears about death. You will be relieved, happier and healthier as you embrace the reality of death, make plans for your own death, and support your loved ones in making their own plans.

Making no plans or preparations means you leave your family overwhelmed and unnecessarily burdened with literally hundreds of details and decisions which must be made at the time of your death if you do not pre-plan. I know of which I speak. This is the voice of experience.

The greatest gift you can give your survivors is to mindfully make plans for your departure from this life. Once the plans and preparations are made, you can relax and enjoy every day. You will be able to say along with the Pulitzer-prize winning poet Mary Oliver and along with me:

"...when death comes...

I want to step through the door full of curiosity,
*   wondering:*
what is it going to be like, that cottage of darkness? ...

And therefore I look upon everything
as a brotherhood and a sisterhood,
and I look upon time as no more than an idea,
and I consider eternity as another possibility,

and I think of each life as a flower, as common
as a field daisy, and as singular,

and each name a comfortable music in the mouth,
tending, as all music does, toward silence,

and each body a lion of courage, and something
precious to the earth.

When it's over, I want to say all my life
I was a bride married to amazement.
I was the bridegroom, taking the world into my arms.

When it's over, I don't want to wonder
if I have made of my life something particular, and real.

I don't want to find myself sighing and frightened,
or full of argument.

I don't want to end up simply having visited this world.

(READ MARY OLIVER'S entire poem at https://tinyurl.com/yda24juz)

MAKING A DIFFERENCE

Appreciating life every day will not only enhance the quality of your life, but will also lighten, brighten, and elevate the collective consciousness. You will be part of neutralizing lower, darker, slower energies that if left unchecked could potentially destroy the planet. By living every day to the fullest, you will be giving a priceless gift to the entire human family.

Chapter 10

PRACTICE SELF-RESPONSIBILITY

YOU ARE THE EXPERT ON YOU

BELOVED READER, YOU KNOW YOUR OWN SELF, YOUR HISTORY, your current situation, your feelings, your beliefs, your temperament, your challenges, your wishes and dreams better than anyone else. *Are you willing to use what you know about yourself to enhance your happiness and health and at the same time raise the collective consciousness?*

IMAGINE, THEN WRITE IT IN YOUR JOURNAL

Assume for a moment that you already know the answers to life's most important questions. Allow yourself the luxury of being still and quiet for a few minutes. Close your outer eyes and breathe gently and deeply several times. Take your time. Let your mind be completely still for a few moments. If thoughts drift in, let them gently drift away.

With your "inner eyes," imagine that you are looking at a huge movie screen that is completely white and blank. Breathe ... breathe ... breathe...Then, ask your Inner Wisdom the question, "What can I do to be happier and healthier?" Notice the first thing that comes to your mind. Trust it. Open your eyes and write it down.

THE COMFORT OF VICTIMHOOD?

Self-responsibility may be the single most important and powerful suggestion contained in this book, though certainly not the easiest or simplest. To accept responsibility for the direction and quality of one's own life means letting go of the convenience and dubious luxury of excuses, procrastination, blaming, and (perhaps most toxic) the comfort of victimhood. *Are you willing to let go of the comfort of victimhood?*

Trust me when I say I reached adulthood having elevated victimhood into a fine art. I had lived my entire life as a child in an environment of neglect, abuse, abandonment and injustice (well-intentioned though perhaps uninformed and misguided.) As an adult I unconsciously sought what was most familiar in interpersonal relationships, i.e. neglect, abuse, abandonment and injustice. I not only tolerated it but looking back I realize I even invited it without being consciously aware that I was doing so.

The familiar was not hard to find. Finding what is familiar is never difficult. We attract it like magnets.

Having attracted people who would willingly treat me the way I was accustomed to being treated, then I had the reward or "payoff" of familiar bad feelings, including worthlessness, despair, self-righteous resentment, self-pity, loneliness, depression, anxiety, cluelessness and confusion in personal relationships, and suicidal ideation. In retrospect, I realize there was a certain "comfort" in the familiarity of these feelings. They reinforced my negative self-image and my fatalistic ideas about life.

I had lived with this pain all my life so I knew better how to live with the pain of neglect, abuse, abandonment, and injustice than how to live with more positive experiences. Someone once said, "I may live in hell, but at least I know the names of the streets."

Thankfully, as a young adult I sought and found numerous sources of help to make changes in the way I thought and in the way I behaved. Over time I learned to value myself equally with other persons (neither "better than" nor "less than," simply equal) and to set and maintain healthy personal boundaries in order to protect the most vulnerable parts of myself without violating others.

Some anonymous wise person said, "Children are victims. Adults are volunteers." For many years this idea helped me to resign from being a volunteer for poor treatment.

Now, I choose to believe that *I was never a victim*, not even as a vulnerable child. Rather I am a spiritual being on a human journey. I choose to believe that I came to this life in order to learn certain life lessons for my soul's evolution. One of the lessons I came here to learn and re-learn and teach is the possibility and process of *transcendence*, or rising above/going beyond/overcoming adversity. Edwene Gaines, one of my most influential spiritual teachers said, "We teach best what we most need to learn."

Every person or institution or situation which has ever given me an occasion to rise above or go beyond or overcome (that is to say, to transcend) has in fact done me a favor and has helped me to evolve in spiritual knowledge, wisdom, strength, and compassion.

For more exploration of this idea, I highly recommend the book *The Little Soul and the Sun: A Children's Parable,* a gorgeously illustrated children's book with an enlightened message for all ages. It is adapted from *Conversations with God,* by Donald Neale Walsch.

You may or may not be ready to consider that you have *never* been a victim. Be that as it may, perhaps you can begin to imagine that as a conscious adult you can choose your reaction to anything that happens to you moving forward and thereby avoid victimhood.

MOVING FORWARD

One simple way to do this is to always ask yourself the question, whatever may come, "What is my lesson in this?" If the obstacle or challenge or difficulty doesn't kill us and we learn something valuable or relearn it at a deeper level, then we are not victims *unless we absolutely insist on being a victim*. We can forgive any transgressor, if we are willing (see previous chapter on forgiveness). Even better for us and for others, we can call anyone who might be called a transgressor an angel sent to help us learn a valuable lesson. Then we move forward with a lesson learned or re-learned and something new to teach.

By the way, if it *does* kill us then we get to experience the next great adventure. We move into that next great adventure not as victims but as overcomers.

EXTRAORDINARY TRANSCENDENCE

I once heard a story of a shop owner who was perpetually positive and cheerful. One evening as he was closing his shop he was shot in a burglary attempt. When help arrived, he was rushed to the hospital and into the operating room. One of the attending hospital staff yelled at him, "Are you allergic to anything?" His eyes popped open and he shouted back, "Yes! Bullets!" Then he laughed and the entire operating room staff laughed with him! The shop owner recovered quickly from his gunshot wound and maintained his perpetual cheerfulness.

This is not to minimize trauma as extreme as being shot by a burglar. This is simply to say that even in the most extreme life-threatening circumstances, we have choices as to how we respond.

Another powerful lesson in self-responsibility is included in the book *Tuesdays with Morrie,* again highly recommended. It is a memoir by American author Mitch Albom about a series of visits he made to his former college professor Morrie Schwartz. Morrie was gradually losing his life to amyotrophic lateral sclerosis or ALS (also called Lou Gehrig's disease). Morrie eventually became completely dependent on his caregivers, bedridden and very much like an infant.

As is typical with ALS, Morrie's sharp mind was unaffected by the disease. He was completely alert and aware. At one point, Morrie tells his visitor Mitch that he has come to enjoy his dependency, even to the point of enjoying being diapered like a baby. Morrie says he appreciates being treated so tenderly and lovingly by those who change his diapers. He died peacefully shortly after.

Your author will confess that being so totally helpless and dependent on others while still being mentally alert is among the worst things I can imagine. I only hope that if I am ever in a similar state, I will respond as courageously and gracefully as Morrie. By all accounts he was an extraordinary teacher in his lifetime and if anything even more influential in his dying. Morrie is one of those who raised the collective consciousness.

You may know of others who have transcended very challenging circumstances without becoming victims. With those in mind and with the examples cited in this chapter, you now have a choice. *Will you accept and embrace responsibility for your life or will you procrastinate, make excuses, blame others or yourself, or otherwise relinquish your power?*

A TRANSCENDENT SOUTHERN WOMAN

One of my favorite she-roes is Helen Keller, an American author, political activist, humanitarian and lecturer. Born in 1880 in Tuscumbia, Alabama, she contracted an illness at nineteen months of age that left her both deaf and blind and therefore unable to learn speech. She lived, as she recalled in her autobiography, "at sea in a dense fog."

Helen's mother searched tirelessly for someone who could help Helen. She eventually found Anne Sullivan (another favorite she-ro of mine). Sullivan was vision impaired herself, which perhaps helped to uniquely qualify her to help Helen. With Sullivan's faithful and determined tutelage, Helen broke through the fog into the light. She learned to communicate and in 1904, at the age of 24, Keller graduated with honors from Radcliffe University, becoming the first deaf-blind person to earn a Bachelor of Arts degree.

Determined to communicate with others as conventionally as possible, Keller learned to speak clearly and spent much of her life giving speeches and lectures on aspects of her life. She learned to "hear" people's speech by reading their lips with her hands—her sense of touch had heightened. She became proficient at using Braille and reading sign language with her hands as well.

In 1916, Keller and Sullivan traveled to the small town of Menomonie, Wisconsin, to deliver a lecture. Details of her talk were provided in the local newspaper. Hopefully, the alert reader will notice how the newspaper accounts illustrate the principles of this book. I have italicized certain phrases and passages of the accounts for emphasis:

A *message of optimism, of hope, of good cheer, and of loving service* was brought to Menomonie Saturday—a message that will linger long with those fortunate enough to have received it. This message came with the visit of Helen Keller and her teacher, (Anne Sullivan), and both had a hand in imparting it Saturday evening to a splendid audience that filled The Memorial. *The wonderful girl who has so brilliantly triumphed over the triple afflictions of blindness, dumbness and deafness, gave a talk with her own lips on "Happiness,"* and it will be remembered always as a piece of inspired teaching by those who heard it.

When part of the account was reprinted a century later in

the January 20, 2016, edition of the newspaper under the heading "From the Files", the column compiler added:

According to those who attended, Helen Keller spoke of the joy that life gave her. *She was thankful for the faculties and abilities that she did possess* and stated that the most productive pleasures she had were curiosity and imagination. *Keller also spoke of the joy of service and the happiness that came from doing things for others ... Keller imparted that "helping your fellow men was one's only excuse for being in this world and in the doing of things to help one's fellows lay the secret of lasting happiness."* She also told of the joys of loving work and accomplishment and the happiness of achievement. Although the entire lecture lasted only a little over an hour, the lecture had a profound impact on the audience.

Keller is remembered as an advocate for people with disabilities amid numerous other causes. She was a suffragette, pacifist, and birth control supporter, at a time when advocacy for women's reproductive rights was considered radical and scandalous.

Her impact on the deaf community was unprecedented. She traveled to twenty-five different countries giving motivational speeches about deaf people's conditions.

In 1915 she and others founded the Helen Keller International (HKI) organization, devoted to research in vision, health and nutrition. In 1920, she helped to found the American Civil Liberties Union (ACLU).

Keller traveled to over 40 countries with Sullivan, including several trips to Japan, and became a favorite of the Japanese people. Keller met every U.S. President from Grover Cleveland to Lyndon B. Johnson and was friends with many famous figures, including Alexander Graham Bell, Charlie Chaplin and Mark Twain.

Keller was inducted into the Alabama Women's Hall of Fame and the National Women's Hall of Fame. In 1964, President Lyndon B. Johnson awarded her the Presidential Medal of Freedom, one of the United States' two highest civilian honors.

In 1999, Keller was listed in *Gallup's Most Widely Admired People of the 20th century.*

If anyone ever had a right to wallow in the comfort and familiarity of being a "helpless victim," perhaps it was Keller. Instead, with help from her mother, her teacher Anne Sullivan and others, she was an overcomer. As the newspaper writer noted, she "brilliantly triumphed over the triple afflictions of blindness, dumbness and deafness," at a time when privileged Southern ladies "knew their place" and kept quiet.

Helen Keller has been widely quoted and one of my favorite quotes from her is this:

> *"Although the world is full of suffering, it is also full of the overcoming of it."*

Helen Keller did not deny the reality of suffering or hardship. She endured her share of it and some might even say more than her share. However, instead of identifying as a victim of suffering, *she chose to focus on the overcoming of suffering* and became an immortal inspiration, leaving a priceless legacy by raising the collective consciousness to benefit all of humankind.

SHOPPING IN EMPTY STORES

Another common trap to avoid self-responsibility is looking for a Rescuer or looking for The Answer(s) outside oneself. Your author certainly spent years looking for Prince Charming and other Rescuers and racing and rushing around to various sources looking for the Answer(s).

I don't really regret that now. I learned many things I needed to know and (as is often said in the fellowship of Alcoholics Anonymous), "it has taken everything I have been through to get me where I am today," which for me is a very good place! However, I am most grateful to those teachers who said, "Love yourself instead of looking for love from outside yourself ... Look within yourself and you will find your answers."

LOOK WITHIN

Beloved reader, the answers are *all* within you. The Cavalry isn't coming. You are the One and the Only One who can take full complete responsibility for your happiness, for your health, and for fulfilling your purpose in life.

Paradoxically perhaps, this doesn't mean you must get to where you want to go completely alone. In fact, we can only get to where we want to go holding hands with one another and helping one another. We all need one another and at the same time, there is a part of your soul's journey that no one else can do for you.

While none of us is self-sufficient, each of us is a competent adult who can form spiritual communities or "mutual aid alliances" with other spiritual beings on a human journey that will help everyone reach their desired goals. *If Helen Keller can learn to do that, what is my excuse?*

MAKING A DIFFERENCE

The opportunity is to practice self-responsibility in partnerships that help us evolve as individual souls and at the same time raise the collective consciousness to improve the planet for today and for future generations. The answers are all within each of us. ... *and* they are most commonly revealed in the context of respectful, loving, mutually affirming spiritual families. Who wouldn't want to be a part of that?

If you always do what you always did, you will always get what you always got. If nothing changes, nothing changes.

UNIVERSAL SPIRITUAL TRUTH

If you do decide to accept responsibility and start doing what you can to co-create a better reality for yourself and others, be assured that *the Universe will take ten or more steps to assist you for every step you take in a positive direction.* I have lived long enough to witness and experience this phenomenon for myself and the Universe does not play favorites. When it comes to universal spiritual truth (such as this), *what is true for any of us is true for all of us.* That is why it is called universal.

A DECISION TO BEGIN...OR NOT

I have been inspired for many years by the following, written in 1951 by the mountaineer William Hutchison Murray and published in his work *"The Scottish Himalayan Expedition."* He wrote a compelling passage about commencing a task, and he finished with a couplet which he attributed to Goethe (bold type added for emphasis):

"Until one is committed there is hesitancy, the chance to draw back, always ineffectiveness. Concerning all acts of initiative (and creation), there is one elementary truth, the ignorance of which kills countless ideas and splendid plans: that **the moment one definitely commits oneself, then Providence moves too. All sorts of things occur to help one that would never otherwise have occurred.** A whole stream of events issues from the decision, raising in one's favour all manner of unforeseen incidents and meetings and material assistance, which no man could have dreamt would have come his way. I have learned a deep respect for one of Goethe's couplets:

**'Whatever you can do, or dream you can, begin it.
Boldness has genius, power, and magic in it.'"**

IN MODERN TIMES parts of the text above have sometimes been directly attributed to the great German playwright and thinker Johann Wolfgang von Goethe. In fact, none of it was written by Goethe. The couplet was from Irish poet John Anster and the rest should be credited to Murray.

Whatever the provenance of the passage, it contains universal spiritual truth relevant to all of us. When we do our part to move forward with commitment and courage (that is to say, being afraid but doing it anyway), *the Universe does its part which is so much bigger and greater than our little part.*

However, the Universe is *always* infinitely respectful of our free will. If we decide (consciously or otherwise) to stay stuck in the same rut where we now are stuck rather than take a step out of it, the Universe will not interfere with or intrude upon our decision. If we insist on staying in the rut, the Universe will support us in staying in the rut. However, if and when we get ready to leave that rut, the Universe will help us get out.

The great American philosopher Henry David Thoreau wrote the following (edited for gender inclusive language):

> *"If one advances confidently in the direction of one's
> dreams, and endeavors to live the life s/he has
> imagined, s/he will meet with success unexpected in
> common hours."*

Are you willing to advance (confidently or not) in the direction of your dreams? What do you really have to lose, except your disillusionment, your despair, your victimhood?

A CHALLENGE

The choice is yours and yours alone. No one can make the decision for you. That power to choose is an amazing and priceless gift and *not to decide is to decide*. I lovingly invite you to make a decision now for bliss and for making a positive difference for all humankind. We need you to be happy and healthy in mind, body, and spirit.

AFTERWORD

Beloved reader, if you have read this far into this manuscript, you are courageous and determined indeed. Only very old, very wise souls read this far into this type of literature. You self-select and self-screen.

In my own personal work and having been a trusted companion for literally thousands of others at a very deep level, it seems to me that there is a point in the journey toward greater conscious awareness and healing that I would describe as "a point of no return." At this point in the journey, there is no longer an option to "go back to sleep" (i.e., go unconscious) and stop moving forward to more enlightenment. We may take a short break to rest and to integrate our experiences before continuing onward, but even the inner process of pausing to integrate is a form of moving forward along the spiraling pathway.

If you have read this far into the manuscript, you are most likely one of those souls who is beyond the point of no return. You no longer have the option of going back into unconsciousness. You know too much. Congratulations!

If you are ready, you can review the ten strategies offered in this volume and choose one or two to play with for a while.

Ideally, find a local, in-the-flesh accountability partner to play with you.

Ancient Eastern wisdom says, "When the student is ready, the teacher appears." If you fully commit yourself to continuing your journey with the Ten Simple Strategies Process, your personal angels will guide you to whatever resource you need in order to succeed.

Remember, success is learning and re-learning lessons and getting up every time we fall down. Success is a journey, not a destination.

Consider joining the "Ten Simple Strategies..." on-line community www.facebook.com/Grace-Terrys-Angels. Consider one-to-one or group coaching with your author and/or with another trustworthy mentor. Schedule an appointment at www.angelsabide.com

I will repeat once more for emphasis:

> As a spiritual being on a human journey, you will accomplish things with accountability and support that you will never accomplish alone. What do you have to lose other than the comfort and questionable rewards of being a victim?

Know that your author supports you 100% *without condition*, no matter what you decide, no matter what you choose to do or not do with "your one wild and precious life" (phrase borrowed from the poem, *"The Summer Day,"* by **Mary Oliver**, 1935-2019, a Pulitzer Prize winning poet). I trust your process.

I am here to support you in myriad ways which we can explore together. Angels attend and abide with you always.

ACKNOWLEDGMENTS

It takes a village to publish a book.
My most sincere gratitude goes to:

My beloved husband, Jim Auxier, who lovingly and faithfully
supports my creative endeavors;

Michael Lacey, formatting and publishing consultant at Story-
Builds.com;

Bogdan Stancu, my cover designer,
bogdan@internetmarketinglight.com

Self-Publishing School, self-publishingschool.com

FINAL NOTE AND REQUEST

A FINAL NOTE AND REQUEST FROM "Amazing Grace" -

THANK YOU FOR READING MY BOOK!

Please go to the www.facebook.com/Grace-Terrys-Angels and give me your honest feedback so that future editions of this book can be improved.

Then, if my message has benefitted you and you honestly think others could benefit from it, please leave a review on Amazon.com.

Your review will help others find me and know that my book is a worthwhile purchase.

Angels abide with you.
   -Grace
   grace@angelsabide.com
   www.angelsabide.com
   www.facebook.com/Grace-Terrys-Angels

ABOUT THE COVER

In 2000, I met Dr. Will Tuttle and his beloved Madeleine when they came to Unity of Louisville and offered a transformational workshop on developing spiritual intuition titled "Opening the Intuitive Gate." They also offered the opportunity to schedule an individual session with them.

I attended the workshop and found it quite meaningful and enlightening. Among other gifts, Will is a virtuoso pianist. I remember the music he incorporated into the workshop was powerful, evocative, and healing, so I scheduled an individual session with Will and Madeleine for the next day in the church's sanctuary.

My session started with the three of us holding hands while Will said a short, simple prayer for divine presence and guidance. He then invited me to just relax on the front pew, breathe, and enjoy the experience. He sat down at the church's grand piano, to which he had connected his recording equipment. Spontaneously and intuitively, Dr. Will composed a gorgeous thirty-minute musical masterpiece uniquely tailored for me!

From the first few chords he played, it was a extraordinary experience. I sat on the front pew and allowed the notes and melodies to surround me and infuse me with serenity. At the same time, Madeleine sat quietly on the other side of the sanctuary with her easel and water colors and spontaneously, intuitively created a painting just for me!

A few minutes into the concert, I decided to close my eyes and allow any inner images evoked by the music to arise before my "inner eyes." A similar imagery practice was one of the experiences of Will's workshop the night before.

I closed my eyes and allowed images to form in my mind without preplanning or effort. I first observed, as if from a short distance, a large antique carousel (or "merry-go-round") with exquisitely carved and painted animal rides. The various animals were rotating around the center of the carousel and gently ascending and descending rhythmically. It was something to see!

After watching from a distance for just a few moments, suddenly I experienced myself as a young child astride one of the beautifully carved and painted carousel horses. With me were my brother and sister, also appearing as they had as young children, each also astride a carousel animal.

Standing beside us and just barely behind us were my mom and dad, holding onto vertical poles with one hand for balance and putting their other hands out to steady the three of us and keep us safe,. They were young and beautiful and healthy. The five of us were all smiling from ear to ear at one another and having the greatest time together riding that carousel.

At the time of this experience, my parents were both deceased. Both of them had died relatively young at ages fifty-six and fifty-eight. In the carousel experience they both appeared as they had in their early thirties, when my siblings and I were all small children.

When I say I experienced myself in this scenario, it was all just as real as anything I have ever experienced in my entire "eyes wide open" life. ... and what I realized and suddenly knew *absolutely* in every cell of my body and beyond, is that **all five of us were as *completely innocent* as the day we were born, *totally without fault or shame* .... And I knew that this**

absolute innocence was the ultimate truth about the essence of each of us. Sitting on that church pew with Will's music transcending time and space, tears streamed down my cheeks as I joyfully embraced this reality.

After a while Will's musical masterpiece came to its perfect conclusion and he stopped playing. I opened my eyes and shakily stood up. Will smiled and handed me both a CD and a cassette tape recording of the masterpiece, which I still have and enjoy to this day.

Madeleine handed me the painting she had completed for me while Will had composed my special music. It was now time for the next scheduled person to come in. I was so overwhelmed by my experience I don't think I could have described it then if there had been time, so I stammered my thanks and dazedly walked out of the sanctuary.

The next day, before Will and Madeleine departed for their next destination, the Universe arranged for Dr. Will and me to have a brief face-to-face conversation. By that time, I was somewhat more grounded and coherent than when I left my session with him the day before. I was able to describe to him what I had experienced on the carousel with my family. Tears shown in his eyes as I thanked him again.

At the time Madeleine showed me the canvas she painted for me, my reaction was something like, "Oh, that's nice...." Although I was delighted with the lovely colors she used and the symbols were aesthetically pleasing, I did not immediately feel connected to it. However, something about it was compelling. I framed the painting and for all these years have hung it in places where I would see it frequently each day. I have peered into its depths countless times.

It was only a short time ago that I realized **the painting IS OF ME!** I am the bridge (or the medium) between heaven and earth. I AM the Tree of Life, which is an ancient interfaith symbol representing physical and spiritual nourishment, transformation and liberation, union and fertility, growth, rebirth/resurrection, and immortality. The wings and spirals in the picture are celestial angels abiding with me.

Way back then, Madeleine could see in me and in my reality what I have only recently begun to see in myself and in my world. Peering deeply into the images helped me to eventually know and claim these powerful truths *about* myself *for* myself and *for others*. I share this with all humility and with the invitation for you to know that these universal truths about me are also true of *you* ... this and so much more.

For obvious reasons, I decided to use Madeleine's painting uniquely created for me for the cover of this book. If you would like to know more about Dr. Will and Madeleine Tuttle and how they are raising the collective consciousness of planet Earth, visit www.willtuttle.com. The couple travels extensively and may soon be in your area. Sign up for their e-newsletter and you will receive regular updates of their itinerary and opportunities for you to enjoy their myriad gifts for yourself. I highly recommend them.

END

Made in the USA
Columbia, SC
14 August 2020